Essential Histories

The Vietnam War
1956–1975

Essential Histories

The Vietnam War
1956–1975

Andrew Wiest

First published in Great Britain in 2002 by Osprey Publishing,
Elms Court, Chapel Way, Botley, Oxford OX2 9LP, UK
Email: info@ospreypublishing.com

Every attempt has been made by the publisher to secure the
appropriate permissions for material reproduced in this book. If
there has been any oversight we will be happy to rectify the
situation and written submission should be made to the
Publishers.

ISBN 1 84176 419 1

Editor: Rebecca Cullen
Design: Ken Vail Graphic Design, Cambridge, UK
Cartography by The Map Studio
Index by Alison Worthington
Picture research by Image Select International
Origination by Grasmere Digital Imaging, Leeds, UK
Printed and bound in China by L. Rex Printing Company Ltd.

02 03 04 05 06   10 9 8 7 6 5 4 3 2 1

For a complete list of titles available from Osprey Publishing
please contact:

Osprey Direct UK, PO Box 140,
Wellingborough, Northants, NN8 2FA, UK.
Email: info@ospreydirect.co.uk

Osprey Direct USA, c/o MBI Publishing,
PO Box 1, 729 Prospect Ave,
Osceola, WI 54020, USA.
Email: info@ospreydirectusa.com

www.ospreypublishing.com

Contents

Introduction

The importance of the Vietnam War

Historians usually judge the Vietnam War to be one of the most important conflicts of the twentieth century. At first glance, though, the significance of the conflict in Vietnam is sometimes difficult to ascertain. The war in Vietnam was, in many ways, small – involving only limited action by a world superpower on distant battlefields of the Third World. During the nine years of official American involvement in the Vietnam War over two million Vietnamese and 58,219 Americans lost their lives. Such numbers truly represent a great tragedy, but pale in comparison to the millions of casualties of the two World Wars. In fact more Americans die every year in traffic accidents than died during the entire Vietnam War. Why, then, is the Vietnam War so important?

The importance of a conflict is gauged not only on casualty figures and geographic spread, but also on the impact that conflict has on the wider world. Using such a scale the conflict in Vietnam ranks as possibly the most important American event of the twentieth century. The war took place during, and became intertwined with, the turbulent 1960s. The volatile mixture of Vietnam, the counter culture, and the Civil Rights Movement led to a near breakdown in the American body politic. In 1968, amid a spate of riots and assassinations, many observers thought that the United States was on the brink of a second American Revolution. The societal tension was so high that the US slowly backed out of a war that

Three US soldiers drag a captured Viet Cong soldier away for questioning in 1966. The brutal nature of the struggle in Vietnam exacerbated societal turmoil on the homefront making Vietnam the most controversial of American wars. (TRH Pictures)

it felt it could no longer win. In the years that have passed since the end of American involvement in the Vietnam War it has become clear that the conflict formed a watershed in American, and certainly Vietnamese, history. Indeed the impact of the Vietnam War was felt worldwide - from the 'Killing Fields' of Cambodia and the ethnic cleansing of Hmong tribesmen in Laos, to social upheaval in Europe and societal discord in Australia over that nation's controversial role in the combat in Vietnam.

The war in Vietnam was also of great importance in a geopolitical sense, as a flashpoint in the Cold War. In the wake of the Second World War the US and the Soviet bloc countries faced off against each other in diplomatic and ideological hostility, while generally avoiding open warfare. Instead the United States chose to counter the perceived threat of the spread of communism across the globe by relying on a system of containment. In each case the scale of the threats precluded the use of massive force, so avoiding the buildup to a nuclear exchange. The US chose to adopt a policy of limited war, hoping to avoid a superpower showdown and in many ways the war in Vietnam became the main example of US limited war policy. It was a war that the United States had to enter in order to contain the spread of communism. It was, however, a war that the United States could not win due to serious limitations placed on the use of American military might. Thus the experiment in limited war failed, coloring all subsequent conflicts from Afghanistan to the Gulf War. However, in some ways Vietnam can be seen as a success. The war did not escalate into a Third World War and, if viewed as only part of the Cold War, one can see a US victory in Vietnam with the eventual fall of the Soviet Union.

The nature of the conflict in Vietnam took the United States by surprise. Trained for battle on the plains of Western Europe, the US military, with its high level of technological developments, found itself involved in a war with Third World guerrilla

fighters. Baffled by the enemy tactics the US military responded, in the main, conventionally, relying on firepower to overcome enemy willpower. Though the US resorted to the heaviest bombing in the history of warfare and won every battle, its tactics were ill suited to overcome what was essentially an insurgency rooted in internal political turmoil. Such military advances as were made during the struggle, including the use of air mobility and the beginnings of electronic warfare, had little impact on the political basis of the conflict. Following the Vietnam War, and despite the 'Revolution in Military Affairs' that saw the technology in warfare progress apace (perhaps best demonstrated in the Gulf War) the military has also come to learn its limitations. Careful not to become enmeshed in a political war the commanders in the Gulf, themselves Vietnam veterans, quickly halted the conflict. Even now, as the war against terror rages, military leaders are careful to ensure that they do not become embroiled in the political chaos of Afghanistan.

Finally, in a much more personal sense, the Vietnam War changed America forever. After the great moral crusade of the Second World War, most Americans were convinced that their country could do no wrong. However, defeat in Vietnam and the attendant social discord of the 1960s, forced a cathartic reappraisal of American society. American soldiers had won every battle, but the war itself had been lost, which indicated a more fundamental failing on the part of America. America, it seemed, could make blunders, could commit atrocities, could lose. In many ways, then, Vietnam forced a reluctant nation to come of age.

One question that often goes unasked lies at the heart of the importance of the Vietnam War and its cathartic effect on American society: "How did the world's greatest superpower fall to defeat at the hands of a Third World insurgent guerrilla force?" The answer to that basic question is as complex as was the Vietnam War itself. Though many at the time saw Vietnam as a simple issue of freedom versus communism the struggle in

Vietnam in fact represented myriad geopolitical, social, and military ideas. Vietnam was one struggle within the Cold War, involving communism, decolonization and the domino theory. It was a guerrilla war, a technological war, a total war, and a limited war. For the US it was a war that it had to enter but which it had no hope of winning,

The Vietnam Veterans War Memorial best represents the continuing pain caused by the Vietnam War. (TRH Pictures)

due in part to the storms that beset its own society. For the Vietnamese, who had lost all the major battles and still remained undefeated, the conflict continued long after the US had exited.

Chronology

1954 **21 July** Signing of the Geneva Accords

1955 **16 July** Diem renounces the Geneva Accords
23 October Diem becomes president and declares the Republic of South Vietnam

1956 **28 April** US Military and Assistance Advisory Group (MAAG) takes over the training of the South Vietnamese armed forces

1957 **October** Fighting breaks out between the forces of Diem and the Viet Minh

1959 **May** North Vietnam begins moving men and supplies down the Ho Chi Minh Trail

1960 **20 December** The National Liberation Front, dubbed the Viet Cong by its adversaries, takes control of the insurgency in South Vietnam

1961 **May** President Kennedy approves sending Special Forces to South Vietnam and approves the "secret war" in Laos

1962 **8 February** MAAG becomes the US Military Assistance Command, Vietnam (MACV) under General Paul Harkins
22 March Launching of the Strategic Hamlet Program

1963 **2 January** Battle of Ap Bac
11 June Thich Quang Duc immolates himself on a Saigon street corner
1 November Diem is overthrown and killed in a military coup

1964 **20 June** William Westmoreland takes over MACV
2–4 August The Gulf of Tonkin Incident
7 August US Congress passes the Gulf of Tonkin Resolution
November–December Viet Cong attacks on American interests in South Vietnam

1965 **February** President Johnson authorizes Operation Flaming Dart bombing raids
2 March US begins Operation Rolling Thunder
8 March First US combat forces arrive at Da Nang
October–November Battle of the Ia Drang Valley

1966 **5–25 November** Operation Attleboro
December Number of US forces in Vietnam reaches 385,000

1967 **8–26 January** Operation Cedar Falls
22 February–1 April Operation Junction City
May–October North Vietnamese siege of marine base at Con Thien
November Battles for Dak To and Hill 875
December US forces reach 500,000

1968 **22 January** 77-day siege of Khe Sanh begins
31 January Tet Offensive begins
28 February Westmoreland requests 206,000 additional troops
16 March My Lai massacre
31 March Bombing north of 20th parallel ceases and Johnson decides not to run for reelection
10 May Peace talks open in Paris

10 June Westmoreland replaced by General Creighton Abrams
26–29 August Riots at Democratic National Convention in Chicago
5 November Richard Nixon elected president

1969 **March** Secret bombings of Cambodia begin
10–20 May The Battle of Hamburger Hill
8 June Troop ceiling in Vietnam reduced by 25,000
3 September Death of Ho Chi Minh
October Largest anti-war demonstrations in US history

1970 **18 March** Prince Norodom Sihanouk overthrown by Lon Nol in Cambodia
1 May US forces invade Cambodia
4 May National Guard troops kill four at Kent State University in Ohio
December US forces in Vietnam down to 335,000

1971 **February–March** Operation Lam Son 719
29 March Lt. William Calley convicted of mass murder at My Lai
December US forces in Vietnam down to 156,800

1972 **30 March–8 April** Nguyen Hue Offensive
6 April Operation Linebacker begins
8 May Nixon announces the mining of Hai Phong harbor

12 August The last US combat unit leaves South Vietnam
22 October South Vietnamese President Thieu rejects peace treaty
18 December Operation Linebacker II begins

1973 **27 January** A peace agreement is signed by the US and North Vietnam
12 February–29 March US POWs come home
21 February A ceasefire agreement is reached in Laos
7 November The US Congress passes the War Powers Act

1974 **9 August** Nixon resigns
December 80,000 people have died during the year, making it the most bloody of the entire conflict.

1975 **January** North Vietnamese forces overrun Phouc Long province
March North Vietnamese forces launch invasion of South Vietnam
24 March North Vietnamese forces launch the Ho Chi Minh Campaign
8–21 April Battle of Xuan Loc
29–30 April Operation Frequent Wind, the evacuation of Saigon
30 April Saigon falls
24 August Pathet Lao forces take control of Laos
December Khmer Rouge forces take control of Cambodia

The Cold War

At the close of the Second World War the United States emerged as a somewhat reluctant superpower. With Western Europe in tatters America, contrary to its history of isolationism, made the conscious decision to stand guard across the world against the new threat of global communism. In 1946 President Harry Truman gave voice to the new geopolitical position of the United States by stating that America would, "assist all free peoples against threats of revolution and attack from without." The world had learned at Munich in 1938 that appeasing dictators was impossible and that the only alternative was the use of brute force. It thus became the policy of the United States to oppose the new archenemy of freedom, the Soviet Union, at every turn. The theory of containment was born and the Cold War began.

The Soviet Union, though battered by war, seemed to pose a direct threat to the United States. Eastern Europe had been overrun by Soviet armies and in the wake of the chaos of war communist revolution haunted the globe – finding fertile ground in the colonial holdings of now weak European powers. To many policy makers in America it seemed that the Soviet Union was strong and that the entire world, whether by direct attack or revolution, was in danger of falling to communism. The geopolitical situation became worse in 1949 when the Soviet Union successfully tested its own atom bomb and the communist forces of Mao Zedong overran China. The rather simplistic American view that communism was monolithic in nature perhaps exaggerated the significance of these events, but American theorists believed that China and the Soviet Union would act together, joined by revolutionaries from Africa to South America in a vast conspiracy to destroy US power around the world.

As the Cold War became a reality the countries of Western Europe struggled to deal with the legacy of the Second World War. France had suffered quick, ignominious defeat in 1940, leaving her Asian colonies easy pickings for Japanese aggression. By 1941 French forces in Indochina had ceded their control of the area to the Japanese and even facilitated the Japanese rule over the countries that would become Vietnam, Laos and Cambodia. When the United States entered the war against Japan the situation in Indochina became complicated. In Europe the US was allied with free French forces, but the French in Indochina were allied with the Japanese enemy. In Vietnam only one group, an umbrella nationalist organization known as the Viet Minh, stood against Japan. Heading the Viet Minh was the charismatic leader Ho Chi Minh, also leader of the Indochinese Communist Party. He and his military commander Vo Nguyen Giap, stood for communism and independence from French colonialism. The United States chose to overlook its obvious differences with the Viet Minh, and aided them in their efforts to harry Japanese forces in the region.

The demise of Imperial Japan presented the Viet Minh with a wonderful opportunity. Before any other allied nations could step into the breach Ho Chi Minh proclaimed the Democratic Republic of Vietnam and drafted a declaration of independence based on the American model, hoping for continued American support. France, though, had different ideas. Still smarting from their defeat, the French needed to reassert their status as a world power and chose to do so in part by taking back their lost colonies in Indochina. As a result, war broke out between the French and the Viet Minh in November 1946. Outnumbered and outgunned, the Viet Minh fled into the

Ho Chi Minh, the architect of revolution in Vietnam.
(TRH Pictures)

countryside and relied on a protracted guerrilla war in an effort to outlast the French. Ho Chi Minh warned the French: "If we must fight, we will fight. You will kill ten of our men and we will kill one of yours. Yet in the end, it is you who will tire."

The French expected to score a quick victory against the Viet Minh, but had not bargained on fighting such a determined enemy, and one willing to absorb tremendous losses in terms of manpower in order to protract the war while waiting for the French to tire. As the war dragged slowly on it presented the United States with a problem. America stood against continued European colonialism and had been the ally of Ho Chi Minh. In the Cold War, though, Asia was but a sideshow. US military theorists consistently expected the

showdown in the Cold War to take place in West Germany. In this predicted cataclysm the US would have to rely on the strength of its NATO partners, including France. The retention of French support in the Cold War was therefore of paramount importance to the US and consequently America abandoned its support of the Viet Minh. After all Ho Chi Minh was a communist leader in a tiny country that mattered little in world affairs. He could be sacrificed.

The French war in Indochina, initially about the re-implementation of colonialism, quickly became a war that the United States had to view in terms of the ongoing Cold War. In 1949 the French established Emperor Bao Dai as an intended puppet leader. From this point on the French could define their war in Vietnam in terms that the United States could not ignore. South Vietnam was an "independent" nation struggling for its freedom against communist aggression. Also in 1949 Ho Chi Minh, who had downplayed his communist affiliations in the past, began to obtain meaningful support for his war from the new communist regime in China. Having already been abandoned by the US, Ho now began to refer to his war as a communist revolution. The terminology of the war in Vietnam had changed, making it a war about containment that America could not allow the French to lose.

The Korean War

On 25 June 1950 the Cold War became hot in Korea and containment was put to the test. In hindsight the wars in Korea and Vietnam were dissimilar and, in the main, unrelated, but the reasoning of the Cold War era would not allow such a conclusion on the part of the United States. Communists in Korea and Vietnam were regarded as part of the greater war, and their attempts at expansion had to be contained. With these beliefs American involvement in the Vietnam War became inevitable. Vietnam could not be allowed to fall, lest containment fail. President Dwight

Eisenhower put the new position of the United States into words in his inaugural address in 1952 when he remarked that, "the French in Vietnam are fighting the same war we are in Korea."

Though the Viet Minh had been bested in most major battles, by 1953 their policy of protracted war had brought considerable success. Having suffered more than 100,000 casualties the French people began to question whether the long war in Vietnam was worth the continued effort and sacrifice. By 1953 the new French military commander in Vietnam, General Henri Navarre, realized that his forces required a great victory of arms against the elusive Viet Minh to rekindle dwindling French national support for the conflict. His plan, dubbed Operation Castor, was designed to lure the Viet Minh into open battle where French forces could destroy them by making use of their firepower edge in artillery and air support. Navarre chose the isolated village of Dien Bien Phu as the place to make his stand. It lay astride the Viet Minh route into Laos, and was so remote that he believed the Viet Minh would not be able to bring substantial numbers of troops or artillery support to bear in the fighting there. In November 1953 the first French troops parachuted into the area and began to fortify the valley, surrendering the surrounding hills to the Viet Minh. The trap had been set, and the overconfident French, supplied only by air, awaited their coming victory.

The Viet Minh, under the leadership of General Giap, though, decided to make the coming battle at Dien Bien Phu their major action of the entire conflict. Giap knew, as did the French, that a superpower conference was scheduled for spring 1954 in Geneva, Switzerland, that would settle the war in Vietnam. Both the Viet Minh and the French desired victory at Dien Bien Phu to strengthen their bargaining position. At Dien Bien Phu a French force of 12,000 men under the command of Colonel Christian de Castries manned a series of defensive fortifications surrounding an all-important airstrip. The Vietnamese spent months

The French colonial presence in Indochina encompassed the modern-day nations of Vietnam, Laos, and Cambodia. For much of the period of French rule Vietnam was divided into Tonkin (northern Vietnam), Annam (central Vietnam) and Cochin China (southern Vietnam). It was around Saigon – dubbed the "Paris of the Orient" – in southern Vietnam that French colonialism was the most pervasive.

bringing their forces through the trackless jungle to prepare for an assault on the French positions. Nearly 200,000 Vietnamese workers did the impossible and manhandled artillery pieces through the difficult terrain, placing them in impenetrable caves on the hills surrounding Dien Bien Phu. Giap also gathered some 50,000 main force troops and 50,000 support troops for the coming attack. French air reconnaissance failed to detect the scale of the Viet Minh buildup, leaving de Castries in a state of shock at the sheer volume of enemy fire that rained down on his troops on 13 March 1954.

The Viet Minh fire quickly knocked out the French airstrip, leaving only parachute drops to supply the defending forces. French counterbattery fire and air strikes were unable to silence the Viet Minh barrage, leaving the defenders of Dien Bien Phu in desperate straits. In April Giap followed up on the continuing siege of Dien Bien Phu with human wave attacks on several of the strong points. French defensive fire, though, took a fearsome toll on the Viet Minh attackers. Amid the carnage Giap decided to revert to more conventional siege tactics. After further constricting the French lines on 1 May Giap launched his final assault. Viet Minh soldiers overwhelmed French firepower with sheer numbers, leading on 7 May to a French surrender. The cost for the Viet Minh had been high, with some 25,000 casualties but the French had suffered a humiliating defeat the very day before the opening of the Geneva Conference.

Though the Viet Minh had won a clear victory over the French and had the support of the Soviet Union and China, the United States stood staunch in the defense of the containment policy at the Geneva talks. In the end the superpowers did not want to risk

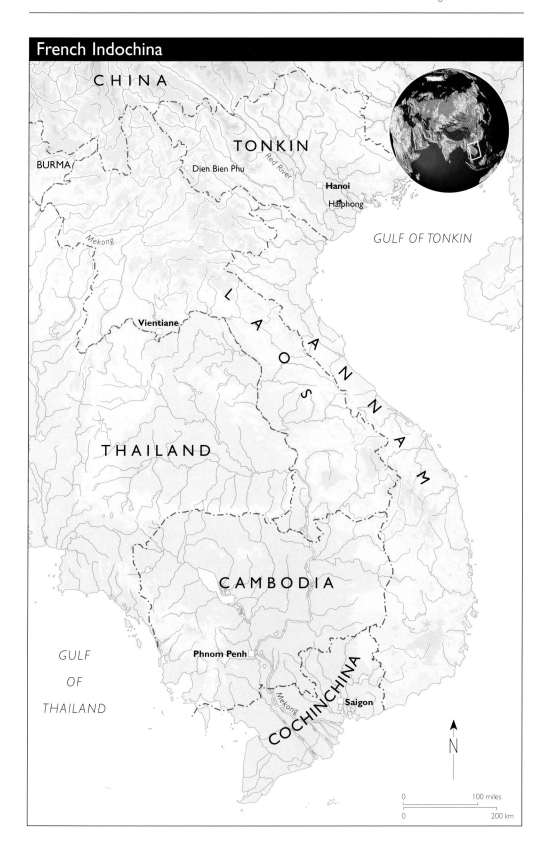

French Indochina

CHINA

TONKIN

BURMA

Dien Bien Phu

Red River

Hanoi

Haiphong

GULF OF TONKIN

L
A
O
S

Vientiane

A
N
N
A
M

THAILAND

CAMBODIA

GULF
OF
THAILAND

Phnom Penh

Mekong

Mekong

COCHINCHINA

Saigon

N

| 0 | 100 miles |
| 0 | 200 km |

US General J. "Lightning Joe" Lawton joins French Colonel Jean de Lattre on a tour of Hanoi – signifying increasing unity with the French. (TRH Pictures)

global war over Vietnam and on 21 July reached an acceptable compromise in the Geneva Accords. The agreement divided Vietnam at the 17th Parallel and established a Demilitarized Zone (DMZ) along that line. The Viet Minh would rule north of the line, and the French would retain control in the south prior to their imminent withdrawal. The border between the two zones would remain open for 300 days to allow people to relocate as they wished. The Geneva Accords specifically stated that the division of Vietnam was not intended to be political in nature or permanent. The country would be reunified by an internationally monitored election in July 1956. Neither Ho Chi Minh nor the Americans were pleased with the compromise. Ho believed that he had won complete victory, but had been abandoned by his erstwhile international allies. He realized, though, that he would easily win the 1956 election and that his victory had only been delayed by two years. The US was upset to lose the northern

half of Vietnam to communism and had no intention of losing the southern half. Thus the US prepared to build and support an independent regime in South Vietnam that could stand firm in support of containment – in violation of the Geneva Accords.

The United States chose Ngo Dinh Diem as the ruler of the new South Vietnam. With CIA support Diem went about the task of solidifying his power base and took control of the Army of the Republic of Vietnam (ARVN), the native force of French colonial origin. A US Military Assistance and Advisory Group took over the task of readying the ARVN for the defense of South Vietnam and American taxpayers paid to structure and equip the burgeoning force. Meanwhile Diem created a constitution for South Vietnam. The democratic document was hardly an effective cover for his dictatorial rule. His was a regime of intense corruption and one that cared but little for the economic well being of the massive Vietnamese peasant population. Though American aid flowed liberally into the country little of it reached the people and poverty haunted the countryside. Thus Diem

French prisoners being led into captivity in the wake of their defeat at Dien Bien Phu. The Viet Minh victory in the battle signified the end of French colonial rule over Vietnam. (TRH Pictures)

did little to earn the support of his own people.

In a military sense the regime appeared to be healthy. Most of the Viet Minh had moved north while the border was open. In addition the communist regime in the north was momentarily weakened by a mistaken effort to implement Stalinist economic reforms. Thus Diem had something of a grace period and Ho Chi Minh could do nothing more than protest when the elections scheduled for 1956 were cancelled. Across South Vietnam Diem's forces hunted down and destroyed the Viet Minh who had remained and by 1958 the communist forces in the South had all but disappeared. Ho Chi Minh, though, remained steadfast in his desire to reunify Vietnam, and in 1959 the

politburo of North Vietnam gave its blessing to an armed uprising in the South. It also directed the foundation of a transportation network through Laos and Cambodia to supply the southern insurgency with men and material – a transportation network eventually dubbed the Ho Chi Minh Trail. Hanoi decided to send south those Viet Minh cadres that had moved north (returnees) as the armed force of the insurgency. Newly trained and equipped these men and women would form the core of the People's Liberation

Armed Force, eventually referred to by their enemies as the Viet Cong. Thus Diem and his ARVN had to face an insurgent guerrilla force that operated as part of a disaffected population, not a communist invasion across the DMZ. For his part Ho Chi Minh realized that he was walking an international tightrope. He wanted to exert

Henry Cabot Lodge, leader of the American Delegation, 25 February 1955. (Topham Picturepoint)

enough military pressure to topple Diem but did not want to draw the United States into the conflict. The Americans, though, could not allow their client state to fall and the road to war began.

Superpower versus guerrilla forces

As war approached in Vietnam it was clear that any military clash between the forces of the United States and North Vietnam would be a classic mismatch. America was the leading world superpower, while North Vietnam was a poor Third World country that had recently fought a long, bitter war and was still involved in a civil war. Nevertheless, several factors served to even the odds in the coming struggle and even provided the North Vietnamese with something of a military edge.

North Vietnam

Ho Chi Minh and Vo Nguyen Giap were the inheritors of a long, martial tradition in Vietnamese history that had seen the Vietnamese nation persevere against all odds numerous times in the distant and recent past. Updating the martial tradition with communist doctrine, Ho decided once again to rely upon the strength of protracted war, in part basing his ideas on the success of Mao's revolution in China. The communists realized that their forces would be at a firepower disadvantage against the Americans or their allies, and thus opted to avoid major battles. Ho realized that time is the one weapon that the weak can use against the strong. The communist plan involved using time and space to create a will to win among their population, while destroying that of their opponents. Revolutionary cadres would blend in with the population, indoctrinating them and launching guerrilla attacks on the superior enemy. After years of effort the foreign power would have to question the worth of

continuing the struggle, exactly as the French had done in 1954. In the end, then, battlefield losses meant little to the communists as long as enemy soldiers died in the process.

The North Vietnamese also had powerful allies in the coming conflict. Tiny North Vietnam, with no viable war economy, could rely on billions of dollars worth of aid from the communist bloc. The aid included the very latest Soviet and Chinese weaponry, from the AK-47 infantry weapon to surface-to-air missiles, although often not in the quantities that the North Vietnamese desired. Without such aid it is doubtful whether the strategy of protracted war would have succeeded in Vietnam at all. Military aid and training served to transform the North Vietnamese Army (NVA) into a world-class fighting force by the early 1960s – a force determined to achieve victory at any cost. For the communists the

Vo Nguyen Giap (center). Choosing to follow the ideals of protracted revolutionary war, Giap would lead North Vietnam's military efforts against both the French and the Americans. (TRH Pictures)

battlefield stretched far beyond the confines of Vietnam. An independent communist insurgency was already taking place in Laos, and the Vietnamese communists made the decision to fight there and in Cambodia as well. For the North Vietnamese the coming war would be a total war calling for national sacrifice and the use of every tactic possible to achieve victory. Facing the challenge of fighting the US the North Vietnamese thus chose to take a rather Machiavellian approach to war, that the end would justify the means.

Initially the communists relied heavily on the forces of the Viet Cong. These fighters, initially southern citizens or returnees, lived and fought as insurgents within the population of South Vietnam. Some men and women joined the Viet Cong due to a true desire for freedom and independence, while others were forced into service by brutal recruitment tactics employed by the communists. By 1968 the number of insurgents in South Vietnam would reach a high of 400,000. Some of the insurgents were members of Viet Cong Main Force units and were professional, full-time soldiers. Many more, though, were in the nebulous category of Viet Cong sympathizer, farmers by day and

To resist the American Air Force bombing over North Vietnam the inhabitants of the Queng Trach constructed trenches leading from each house into the center of the village. The Viet Cong, lightly armed and highly motivated, proved able to stand against the military might of the United States. (TRH Pictures)

soldiers by night. Lightly armed and poorly trained these civilian/soldiers carried out intelligence gathering, nuisance attacks and placed the booby traps that would come to epitomize the conflict. The Viet Cong initially faced off with the ARVN for control of the countryside, but would also play a major role in the war against the United States through the time of the Tet Offensive. As southerners the Viet Cong were often at odds with the northern leadership – but the common antipathy toward the American client state in the South held the two forces together. In addition the rather inept and dictatorial rule of the South Vietnamese regime and the ineffectiveness of the ARVN made the task of the Viet Cong much easier. By 1965 the Viet Cong controlled nearly 60 percent of the South Vietnamese countryside and would continue to do so for most of the war there – giving rise to the American saying, "We rule the day, but Charlie rules the night."

The ARVN

At first communist forces were pitted against the military of the regime in Saigon, the ARVN. Though often derided as an ineffective fighting force, the ARVN struggled against the Viet Cong and the NVA for over 15 years, eventually losing some 130,000 dead and 300,000 wounded. Thus for the ARVN the Vietnam War was much longer and more costly than that of their better-known American allies. Properly trained and equipped ARVN soldiers matched the skill and tenacity of their communist foes – after all both forces came from the same martial stock. However, the ARVN command structure and indeed South Vietnam itself was fatally flawed. The political leaders of South Vietnam, who were often engaged in bitter power struggles among themselves, were extremely corrupt and relied on a military patronage system that was, at best, counterproductive. Upper echelon ARVN commanders were often more interested in political advancement than military victory. In addition the Saigon regime never undertook meaningful land reform, leaving much of the vast peasantry destitute and easy targets for Viet Cong recruitment efforts.

Amid governmental chaos and societal disaffection it is surprising that South Vietnam produced so many men willing to defend their nation at the cost of their own lives. At its peak strength the ARVN numbered nearly one million men. Of that number 450,000 troops served in the Regular Army and often fought with great distinction. The remainder of the South Vietnamese military consisted of less reliable Regional and Popular Forces who often operated in rural areas fighting a bitter "land war" for control of rice production with the Viet Cong. Belittled by western historians, and the forgotten heroes of a country that no longer exists, the ARVN served in every major battle of the Vietnam War – from the Ia Drang Valley to Hamburger Hill – often fighting the lauded NVA to a standstill. For the ARVN to be successful, though, South Vietnam itself had to grow as a nation and overcome its political faults.

Though the ARVN was far from perfect, its raw materials were good. The main problems of South Vietnam were very much political ones. In short a true nation had to be built there: a nation that earned the loyalty and support of its own people and their continuing military sacrifice. To the United States, though, the problem in South Vietnam was seen as military in nature and treated in the main as such – leaving the political and societal flaws of South Vietnam untended until it was too late.

Simply put US leaders believed that the 17th Parallel had to be held against communist expansion and regarded this as a military problem. This oversimplification of the nature of the conflict in Vietnam did much to injure the chances of American and South Vietnamese victory. To Americans the threat of communist expansion was very real. John Kennedy, the new US President, had found out how serious the Cold War was through the Berlin crisis of 1961, the Bay of Pigs fiasco in Cuba in April 1962 and several communist uprisings across the globe. After a tense meeting with Soviet Premier Nikita Krushchev in Vienna Kennedy remarked, "now we have a problem in trying to make our power credible, and Vietnam is the place."

In the paranoid world of the Cold War, Kennedy, and later Lyndon B. Johnson, could

Members of the Viet Cong run to fend off an air attack. (TRH Pictures)

A Viet Cong nurse stands in a rice paddy in the Mekong Delta. She was taken prisoner with 11 guerrillas by a unit of the 44th Vietnam Rangers battalion. The presence of women on the battlefield often presented American forces with a difficult moral dilemma. (TRH Pictures)

not see Vietnam fall to communism. But war in that distant land seemed a tremendous gamble with the fate of the whole world. Vietnam was a communist client state. Too much pressure applied against the North Vietnamese might force the Chinese as in Korea, or lead to a showdown much like the Cuban Missile Crisis of 1962. Nobody in Washington wanted a thermonuclear war over Vietnam, but most believed that a true effort to defeat the communists in North Vietnam would result in a third world war. Also US military thinkers kept part of their attention squarely focused on events in Europe. There was always the chance that the budding conflict in Vietnam was just a ruse, designed to divert American attention and forces from West Germany, where most analysts in the US thought the next world war would be fought. Thus for many reasons the US had to enter the conflict in Vietnam and halt world communism in its tracks. However, the United States could not use all of the military force at its disposal, or attempt to win a true military victory against the North Vietnamese lest the conflict should escalate to nuclear war.

The United States

At the outbreak of the Vietnam War the United States possessed the world's finest armed force. The US armed forces were trained for and fully capable of conducting a war on the continent of Europe against the nations of the Warsaw Pact. On paper, then, the US was at a staggering advantage over the NVA and the Viet Cong. The US, though, chose to fight a limited war in Vietnam with enough effort initially only to prevent the fall of the beleaguered Saigon regime. As more and more returnees came down the Ho Chi Minh Trail with their new weaponry and training, South Vietnam became less and less stable. Unable and unwilling to destroy North Vietnam or reform the government of South Vietnam, Kennedy countered with a graduated escalation of US involvement in the war there. At the beginning of his presidency there had been 650 US advisors in South Vietnam; there were 16,700 at the time of his assassination in 1963. America crept toward a war designed only to retain the status quo.

Even after the war became a more formal affair for the United States in 1965, the American use of armed force remained limited. As the war theorist Carl von Clausewitz postulated, war tends to escalate toward the paradigm of totality. US military thinkers were very aware of this tendency and realized that such a result would mean nuclear war, an unacceptable risk to be run for the sake of South Vietnam. Thus one of the most important goals of US involvement in the Vietnam War was to stop the war from escalating. Achieving this goal involved a conscious restraint in the use of American military force. Toward this end US forces would not engage in an invasion of North Vietnam, Laos or Cambodia. Though there would be clandestine operations in all three areas they were not of the type designed to win ultimate victory. The Americans also placed severe restrictions on the use of their airpower advantage, leaving several of the most important targets in North Vietnam "off limits" in an effort to placate the Soviets and the Chinese.

In Vietnam, then, the communist forces would only face a fraction of America's military might. In addition the US military forces in the area were under severe restrictions as to the use of their firepower, leaving the communists critical safe havens for operations. American forces found themselves facing an insurgent, guerrilla force within the confines of South Vietnam, one that could escape to its safe havens almost at will. The second major goal of the American use of force in South Vietnam was to prevent the collapse of that nation. Victory in such a conflict defied definition or a time schedule – there was no exit strategy. Only the continued survival of South Vietnam would provide the proof of victory. Most strategists in the US, though, believed that the concentrated use of firepower would make short work of the Viet Cong and that attriting the insurgents would solve the problems of South Vietnam. Thus first ARVN and later US forces became involved in a limited war designed to hunt down and destroy the Viet Cong insurgents in a contest of attrition. Such a war played into the hands of the communists, who positively welcomed a protracted war of attrition. Thus doctrine and planning served to tip the military balance in the Vietnam War toward the communists. Though it was a mismatch on paper the Vietnam War was destined to be fought on terms dictated by the NVA and the Viet Cong.

A war of many flags

Though often remembered as an "American War" the conflict in Southeast Asia involved fighting and sacrifice on the part of several nations. As a truly regional conflict the Vietnam War also encompassed related struggles in both Cambodia and Laos – wars that involved "secret" fighting on the part of the world superpowers.

In Vietnam itself, several nations allied to the United States played an active role in the struggle. In 1964 President Lyndon B. Johnson called for the nations of the free world to assist the government of South Vietnam in an alliance of "Many Flags." Over 39 nations

across the globe answered the call. Most countries, including Japan and the United Kingdom restricted their efforts to economic and humanitarian aid. However, four nations – Australia, New Zealand, Thailand, and the Republic of Korea – chose to send combat forces to South Vietnam. The Thais, suspicious of communist intentions in the region, first sent troops to the aid of South Vietnam in 1967. Their involvement in the conflict would reach a peak in 1968 with the dedication of an entire division, dubbed the Black Panthers, to the war. Thai forces were also heavily involved in the fighting in Laos, and US air power made use of several critical Thai airbases including the massive complex at U-Tapao.

The Republic of Korea, anxious to cement relations with the United States, sent combat troops to South Vietnam as early as February 1965 and by the close of 1969 there were over 47,000 Korean troops in Vietnam. Though their forces fought with great ferocity, especially the elite Capital Division, relations between Korea and the United States would soon sour in part due to the fact that the Korean government demanded and received tremendous financial support for their military efforts. Additionally the Koreans never felt that they were treated as an equal partner by their superpower ally.

The governments of Australia and New Zealand, were sensitive to growing communist power in the Pacific, and in early 1962 the Australian Army Training Team Vietnam arrived in South Vietnam to train the ARVN in the art of jungle warfare. By 1966 the Australian commitment to the war had risen to the deployment of two battalions known as the 1st Australian Task Force. Anxious not to be subordinate to US command and control the Australians, with an attachment of New Zealand troops, pressed for and received their own area of operations in the Phuoc Tuy Province southeast of Saigon. Australian and New Zealand forces performed well in combat, partly due to their innovative ideas of counterinsurgency. However, the Vietnam War would become controversial in Australia leading to acrimonious debate that continues to this day.

An undeclared war

By 1963 it was becoming increasingly clear to American observers that the Viet Cong was winning the war in South Vietnam. The weakness of the Vietnamese regime was best expressed in the Battle of Ap Bac, fought in January 1963. Intelligence had located a VC contingent of some 300 men, and under the direction of US advisor Lieutenant Colonel John Paul Vann the ARVN closed in for the kill. Outnumbering the enemy 5 to 1 and possessing a critical edge in firepower and air support the ARVN planned to surround and annihilate the VC force. The Viet Cong, manning strong defensive emplacements, fought well, but the ARVN did not. Hampered by ineffective command at the very highest levels ARVN forces on the ground quickly lost control of the battle and an effort to augment their forces in the field led to the loss of five helicopters. The Viet Cong resisted stubbornly against the poorly coordinated assault and then fled into the night. What should have been an easy victory was at best a costly draw.

The failure of Ap Bac was of critical importance for the future of the conflict. President Diem had hamstrung his own forces by ordering them not to take heavy casualties in an effort to avoid controversy. Thus the South Vietnamese regime was more concerned with its own power than a pursuit of victory. The failure at Ap Bac also demonstrated to the United States that the South Vietnamese regime was corrupt and incapable of defending containment on its own. A major change in US policy appeared to be warranted. Finally the conclusion of the battle did much to set the groundwork for a continuing struggle between the US military and the media that would come to personify the Vietnam War. The military, led by General Paul Harkins, Commander of the US Military Assistance Command, Vietnam,

portrayed Ap Bac as a victory. Senior US reporters in the area, including Neil Sheehan and David Halberstam, though, realized that Ap Bac was a debacle and reported it as such. Thus the gulf between the media and the US military in Vietnam came into being.

As 1963 wore on the situation in South Vietnam worsened. President Diem, a Catholic, unwisely attempted to repress the religious rights of Buddhists in Vietnam, who made up over 80 percent of the population. The most visible sign of these troubles for the outside world came on 11 June, when an elderly Buddhist monk, Thich Quang Duc, immolated himself on a Saigon street corner before representatives of the world media. The images shocked the world, and did much to discredit the Diem government. By August US leadership in South Vietnam, including ambassador Henry Cabot Lodge, had come to support an overthrow of the Diem regime. In November, with US support, the coup plotters took control and assassinated Diem. It was hoped that the new military leadership in South Vietnam would prosecute the war against communism with more vigor and carry out needed social reforms. Such was not the case. Much like Diem the Saigon leadership for the remainder of the war was more concerned with self-preservation and corruption than the construction of a viable nation and the achievement of military victory. The South Vietnamese leadership knew its valuable position; no matter what they did the US could not allow them to be defeated, leaving the ARVN to struggle to defend a chaotic political system in a nation divided against itself.

The assassination of John F. Kennedy brought to power the US president who was to stamp his personality on the Vietnam War: Lyndon B. Johnson. A consummate

The Buddhist monk Thich Quang Duc immolates himself on a Saigon street corner in protest at the attempted suppression of the rights of Buddhists in South Vietnam. (TRH Pictures)

Washington insider, Johnson found himself at the head of a nation united. Johnson chose to utilize the great national consensus for a variety of social programs that he termed the "Great Society," including welfare, medicare, and civil rights. What Johnson did not want was a controversial war that interrupted the consensus for social change. As a Democrat he realized that he had to be tough on communism, and as a believer in Cold War theory he also realized that the US had to contain communist expansion at the 17th Parallel. Finally Johnson was and would remain quite frightened of the possibility of a superpower clash over Vietnam. Thus the distracted new president realized that he had to make a stand in Vietnam – but one that would not cause controversy or an overreaction on the part of the Soviets.

In the presidential election of 1964 Johnson said, "We don't want our American boys to do the fighting for Asian boys. We don't want to get involved in a nation with 700 million people and get tied down in a land war in Asia." While carrying the mantle of the peace candidate, though, Johnson took the first steps toward war. On 2 August North Vietnamese patrol boats attacked the US destroyer *Maddox* in the Tonkin Gulf. Little damage was done and Johnson realized that US forces in the area were involved in covert missions against the North Vietnamese coast. As a result the US did not strike back, but chose to add the destroyer the *C. Turner Joy* to the patrols in the area. In a confused action on the stormy night of 4 August the US forces engaged what they thought to be a renewed North Vietnamese attack. Though the issue of whether the North Vietnamese had attacked at all remained in considerable doubt, Johnson chose to retaliate and ordered Operation Pierce Arrow – the retaliatory bombing of North Vietnamese coastal facilities.

The Ho Chi Minh Trail

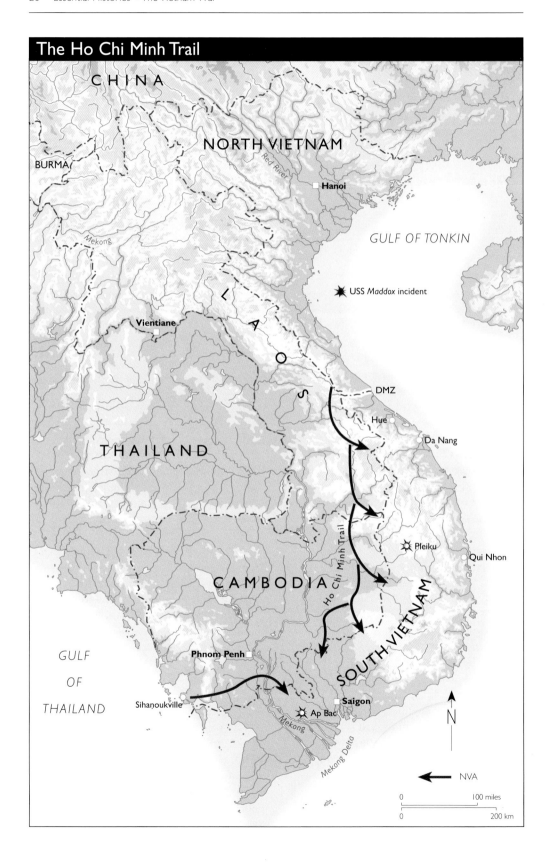

Beginning in 1960 the North Vietnamese made use of political instability in Cambodia and Laos for construction of the Ho Chi Minh Trail – the logistic support line for the burgeoning war in the south. Over several years the trail was transformed into a complex road network and even enjoyed the use of a deep-water seaport at Sihanoukville in Cambodia. The trail, though in "neutral" territory, became the focal point of major US interdiction efforts throughout the war.

The following day Johnson and his chief advisor, Secretary of Defense Robert McNamara, introduced the Gulf of Tonkin Resolution for debate in the US Congress, where he characterized the North Vietnamese attacks as unprovoked aggression. The Resolution was quite broad in scope, allowing the President, "to take all necessary steps, including the use of armed force," in the defense of South Vietnam and its allies. Johnson promised that the Resolution would not be used to start an undeclared war in South Vietnam, and he was telling the truth. He believed that the Resolution itself, coupled with the bombing of North Vietnam, would demonstrate American resolve to support South Vietnam and bring Ho Chi Minh to his senses. Believing that America had been attacked and that Johnson would live up to his promise of peace the Senate and the House of Representatives passed the Gulf of Tonkin Resolution with only two dissenting votes.

Johnson had been given the free hand he wanted in South East Asia, and the US Congress had surrendered its constitutional authority to declare war. The seeds of controversy, however, had been sown. Johnson would use the Gulf of Tonkin Resolution to fight an undeclared war in South Vietnam in violation of his promises. Many US lawmakers, led by the powerful chairman of the Foreign Relations Committee Senator William Fulbright, felt betrayed and would turn against the Vietnam War. In addition as the truth of the fighting in the Gulf of Tonkin came out a credibility gap began to widen between the President and the public.

To the North Vietnamese the Gulf of Tonkin Resolution appeared to be tantamount to a US declaration of war. As a result Ho and Giap chose to redouble their efforts in support of the Viet Cong and for the first time began to target American forces for attack. From November through February the VC pressed their advantage across South Vietnam, and launched terror attacks against US forces, culminating in a 7 February attack on the US airfield at Pleiku. Through such means the communists hoped to convince the US that continued support of South Vietnam would be costly in terms of American lives. Responding to this provocation, US presidential advisors, including McGeorge Bundy, urged Johnson to begin a sustained bombing campaign of North Vietnam to halt the imminent fall of the tottering South Vietnamese regime.

On 13 February a reluctant Johnson gave the go ahead for Operation Rolling Thunder and on 2 March the first bombs struck North Vietnam. The bombing was conceived as a campaign of graduated escalation that would prove an active deterrent against North Vietnamese support for the insurgency in the south. This demonstration of US willpower was intended to bring North Vietnam to its senses and to the bargaining table, obviating the need to send US ground forces into South Vietnam. In the end Rolling Thunder lasted three years and formed the most massive strategic bombing campaign in military history. The campaign was, though, misguided. For fear of provoking the Soviet Union and China US planners limited the targeting of Rolling Thunder and thus limited its effectiveness. In addition North Vietnam was a pre-industrial country and as such was not an effective target for a strategic bombing campaign. The North's war supplies came, in the main, from its communist allies, who the American bombers could not reach. Although the US dropped over 643,000 tons of bombs on North Vietnam, the return on the investment was negligible. Estimates by 1967 suggested that it cost the US $9.60 to inflict $1.00 worth of damage. In addition the fighter-bombers that carried out the bulk of the bombing stood only a 50 percent chance

A Douglas A I E Skyraider drops napalm in a strike on the Ho Chi Minh Trail as part of Operation Rolling Thunder. Though the bombing of North Vietnam was quite intense, it had little impact on the ultimate outcome of the conflict. (TRH Pictures)

of surviving their one-year tour of duty. The prodigious bombing did little to stem the tide of men and materiel headed south on the Ho Chi Minh Trail, and North Vietnamese leaders rallied their population against the "American aggression."

The beginning of Rolling Thunder did little to affect the ongoing fighting in South Vietnam. The Viet Cong continued to press the ARVN back ever further. The new commander of MACV, General William Westmoreland, now had an additional concern as well. Increasingly the US based its air forces engaged in Rolling Thunder at airfields within the confines of South Vietnam. These bases, Westmoreland

realized, made obvious targets for VC attack and were only defended by what he considered to be substandard ARVN units. As a result Westmoreland requested two battalions of Marines to defend the US airbase at Danang. Though some of Johnson's advisors, notably Maxwell Taylor, disliked the idea, Johnson saw the request as reasonable. With little fanfare and little realization of the change it portended Johnson approved Westmoreland's troop request. On 8 March 1965 the Marines landed at Danang. Their presence in South Vietnam illustrated the failure of American policy there. Since 1954 the US had been trying to establish a South Vietnam that could stand on its own in defense of containment. The mere presence of US ground forces showed that the efforts of 11 years had been a failure. American involvement in the Vietnam War had begun.

Battles of attrition

Strategies

Though the Vietnam War had been years in the making, in many ways the final commitment of US combat forces to defend South Vietnam had come as something of a surprise to Johnson and his advisors. The newly arrived force had as its goal the defense of the US base at Danang and the continued independence of South Vietnam. However, there were no distinct plans or even a truly concrete idea in the minds of the administration or the military concerning how to achieve those goals. Westmoreland welcomed the commitment of US troops but felt that many more were needed. The US maintained important, vulnerable bases all over South Vietnam and he also expected a major ground offensive from North Vietnam. For these reasons he immediately increased his request for troops, and by June 1965 the American troop ceiling in Vietnam had been raised to 220,000, a considerable jump in only four months.

Johnson did not want his war in Vietnam to damage the great consensus for social change. He also realized that a full mobilization of US troops would be provocative in terms of the Cold War. Thus Johnson chose not to call up the National Guard or trained reserve, relying instead on a draft system to provide troops for the growing war. This decision was one of Johnson's greatest blunders, for the draft was riddled with loopholes allowing the privileged to avoid military service, and became a lightning rod for national criticism of the conflict in Vietnam. In addition the US military opted for a one-year tour of duty in Vietnam in an effort to limit the exposure of soldiers there to the effects of combat. This well-intentioned move also backfired. After the initial troop deployment soldiers

rotated into and out of Vietnam singly, joining units as replacements and leaving when their tour was up, a practice that destroyed institutional memory and small unit loyalty in Vietnam. A soldier joined a unit of veterans that he did not know, and toward the end of his tour he would become a victim of "short timer's fever." As a result, for many men the war in Vietnam was one of solitary desperation and they sought simply to survive for a year and then return home. Nevertheless, the vast majority of Vietnam era draftees fought with dogged determination and great gallantry.

However, in 1965 the problems of Johnson's military system were in the future. Westmoreland had the finest military in the world and had to develop a plan to defeat the communist enemy. His strategic choices were limited by Johnson's decision to confine US ground forces to South Vietnam. Under these frustrating restrictions Westmoreland hit upon a rather simple strategy to win the war. He planned to destroy the Viet Cong insurgency by wiping out their military cadres using the tactics of "find, fix and finish." Knowing that the enemy was elusive, Westmoreland planned to locate enemy forces using superior intelligence. Then operational mobility would enable US forces to surprise the unsuspecting communists and lock them into battle. Once engaged, US forces could call down the might of their massive artillery and air support to destroy their foe. Westmoreland believed that the annihilation of a few enemy units would show the North Vietnamese the error of their ways, thus allowing South Vietnam to exist in peace. He hoped that victory could be won and American forces withdrawn within three years.

America thus chose to fight a conventional war in Vietnam believing that the application of superior force would achieve victory. Unfortunately, Johnson, not only understood little about the tenacity and dedication of the Vietnamese people, he also overestimated the ability of his own nation to withstand a protracted war. Ho and Giap once again chose to rely upon a drawn out war of attrition to wear down the will of a superior enemy. Communist forces would avoid major confrontations with US units and would instead rely on guerrilla tactics. Such action would cause the continuous, slow loss of American life in Vietnam. Over time, and with ample media coverage, the cumulative effect of the continued losses would make the United States question the value of its war in Vietnam.

The battle of the Ia Drang valley

In 1965 US and North Vietnamese military leaders were both looking to engage the other in battle, partly to learn each other's strengths and weaknesses. For his part Westmoreland expected a communist attack in the Central Highlands near Pleiku on Route 19 designed to cut South Vietnam in two. The rugged terrain there seemingly gave the elusive enemy the edge – but Westmoreland was prepared. At nearby An Khe the 1st Air Cavalry stood ready to use air mobile tactics for the first time. The unit could use its 435 helicopters to carry soldiers into battle nearly anywhere in Vietnam with great speed. Lavish fire support from artillery, helicopter gunships and aircraft ensured that the 1st Air Cavalry would pack quite a punch. This quick-moving, powerful force seemed to negate any possible terrain or mobility advantage the communists might seek to utilize.

Giap, and the NVA local commander General Ghu Huy Man, on 19 October obliged Westmoreland by launching an attack on the US Special Forces camp at Plei Me involving the 320th and 33rd NVA regiments. The offensive was designed in part to seize Pleiku, but it was also designed to draw the Americans into battle. The communists realized that they were facing a

formidable foe and had to learn the American way of war. To Westmoreland the attack on Plei Me presented a wonderful opportunity. The elusive enemy had been located in great strength and could now be fixed into battle for an attritional victory. Seizing his opportunity the US commander ordered the 1st Air Cavalry to hunt down and destroy communist forces in the area in the first test of air mobility.

Having been checked at Plei Me the NVA forces had retreated to the mountain fastness of the Chu Pong Massif surrounding the Ia Drang Valley. On 14 November the two forces met in pitched battle. Helicopters bearing elements of the 1st Battalion, 7th Cavalry, commanded by Lieutenant Colonel Harold Moore, assaulted Landing Zone (LZ) X-Ray at the foot of the Chu Pong massif – inadvertently landing in the midst of the NVA staging area. Even before the entire battalion arrived two NVA regiments, the 66th and 33rd moved to surround the LZ and annihilate the tiny American force. As the battle raged helicopters brought in reinforcements under fire – but the Americans remained severely outnumbered. In savage, sometimes hand-to-hand, fighting the NVA nearly overran the American position, but were defeated by a murderous combination of small arms fire and artillery and air support. For three days the fighting raged around LZ X-Ray, which was no larger than a football field.

It was in the Battle of the Ia Drang Valley that US forces for the first time used their massive B-52 bombers, each carrying 36,000 pounds of high explosive, in a tactical role. Under the hail of fire on 16 November the North Vietnamese chose to break off their attack and retreat into the safe haven of Cambodia. Soon thereafter US forces also retreated from LZ X-Ray to make way for additional B-52 strikes. During this phase of the battle the 2nd Battalion, 7th Cavalry was ambushed and nearly destroyed while making its way to LZ Albany. Sporadic fighting in the area took place until 26 November when the Battle of the Ia Drang Valley officially reached its

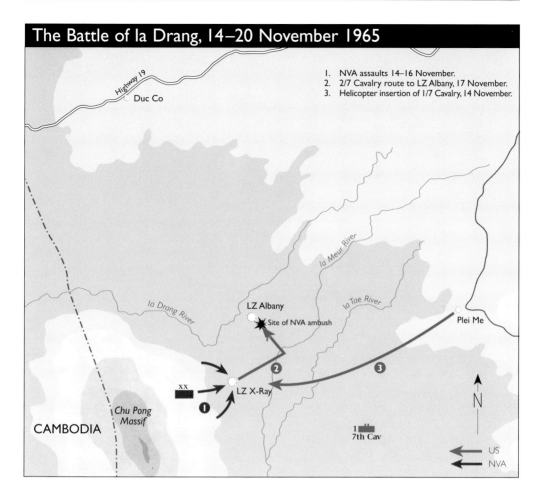

The Battle of Ia Drang, 14–20 November 1965

1. NVA assaults 14–16 November.
2. 2/7 Cavalry route to LZ Albany, 17 November.
3. Helicopter insertion of 1/7 Cavalry, 14 November.

Highway 19
Duc Co
Ia Meur River
Ia Drang River
LZ Albany
Site of NVA ambush
Ia Tae River
Plei Me
LZ X-Ray
XX
Chu Pong Massif
CAMBODIA
1 7th Cav
N
US
NVA

conclusion. During the struggle US forces had lost 305 dead. The NVA, though, had suffered greatly at the hands of US firepower losing an estimated 3,561 dead of a total force of 6,000.

The Battle of the Ia Drang Valley was of critical importance as it set the precedent for the conduct of the war in Vietnam. The air mobility concept had proved its worth. In addition Westmoreland believed that the Ia Drang validated his strategy of attrition, for American forces had inflicted an 11:1 loss ratio upon the NVA. The US commander reasoned that it would not take many more such victories to push the communists to the brink of total defeat. The communists, though, took quite different lessons from the battle. Though they had taken heavy losses the NVA, led by Giap, believed the Ia Drang to be something of a victory because they learned that they could

The first major confrontation between US and NVA forces began on 14 November 1965 and pitted two battalions of the 1st Cavalry against more than 6,000 enemy soldiers amid triple canopy rainforest and a sea of elephant grass. Attacking from prepared defenses on the Chu Pong Massif the NVA forces nearly destroyed the US defenders of LZ X-Ray. However, the first use of air mobile tactics and massive firepower support drove the NVA back to its havens in Cambodia – thus setting the precedent for much of the fighting to come in the Vietnam War.

in fact fight the Americans. The losses, though, convinced Giap to revert to a reliance on guerrilla warfare designed to inflict losses on the Americans before fleeing into Cambodia when their own losses became prohibitive. The tactical initiative lay with the communists. Even when facing air mobility it was the communists who decided whether to stand and fight or to flee to their safe havens, which gave them a critical edge in the conflict.

President Johnson and General William Westmoreland, who saw the war in Vietnam as a simple war of attrition against an outmatched enemy. (Corbis)

In addition the NVA and the VC began to adopt the policy of "hanging on to American belts." This policy called for communist fighters to get as close as possible to US forces before opening fire. If they were in close enough the US would refrain from using lavish artillery and air support for fear of hitting their own troops. Thus Giap sought to avoid further Ia Drangs even as Westmoreland sought to replicate his victory there.

Other aspects of the Battle of the Ia Drang Valley would go on to play a major part in the war and its controversial nature on the American home front. After the close of the battle US forces returned to their base camp at An Khe, thereby setting a pattern. US forces in Vietnam did not seize and hold enemy territory. Thus victory in the Vietnam War became more difficult for the American public to understand. Anxious relatives at home could not track the advance of US forces on a map. There were no breakouts from St. Lo or Inchon landings, instead victory in Vietnam came to be judged in terms of "body count." Though US forces would win every battle in the Vietnam War in these terms, to the American public it seemed that their troops fought again and again in the same places, taking no land and seemingly making no progress. Support for the conflict would begin to wane.

Search and destroy

Though the problems that plagued South Vietnam and the ARVN were political and economic in nature, the US concentrated on military solutions and made ready to fight a "big unit" war in a Third World country – placing only limited emphasis on techniques of counterinsurgency . Likewise NVA and VC forces made ready to face the enemy by bringing more supplies down the Ho Chi Minh Trail and by preparing potential battlefields across South Vietnam with mines, bunker complexes and networks of tunnels. It was not until the fall of 1966 and the onset of Operation Attleboro that US forces made a bid to destroy communist strength in South

Vietnam through a series of search and destroy missions. During October some 22,000 allied forces, including elements of the 1st Division, the 25th Division, the 173rd Airborne and the ARVN swept into War Zone C in Tay Ninh Province near the border with Cambodia. War Zone C, along with the Iron Triangle and War Zone D, was a VC staging and base area just over 40 miles north of Saigon.

Although the month-long operation saw several pitched battles US and ARVN forces never succeeded in locking the 9th VC Division into battle. Using their tactical initiative the VC fought, often on carefully prepared battlefields, until their losses reached an unacceptable level and then broke off the engagement and fled to their safe havens. During Operation Attleboro US forces killed some 1,100 VC while suffering under 100 fatal casualties. In addition US forces wrecked several VC staging areas and drove the VC into Cambodia. To Westmoreland and MACV Attleboro seemed to be an attritional victory, and Westmoreland made ready to launch several such operations in an effort to end the war in 1967. To Ho, Giap, and the communist leadership, though, such a rate of attrition was acceptable. Time and manpower were their main weapons, and they believed that even though the numbers ran 10:1 against them it would be the US that would tire of the Vietnam War first. Also at the close of the operation US forces exited War Zone C, and the Viet Cong returned to the area to rebuild and nurse their wounds.

At the beginning of 1967 Westmoreland had 390,000 US forces at his disposal to administer the death blow to the Viet Cong. In January 1967 over 30,000 US and ARVN forces launched Operation Cedar Falls, designed to destroy VC control over the Iron Triangle. Achieving tactical surprise on 8 January 60 transport helicopters landed in the VC village and base area of Ben Suc. Within minutes the village had been secured and the population removed in an effort to deny support to the local insurgents. For the next three weeks soldiers, including many from the 1st Division and the 173rd Airborne,

swept through the Iron Triangle attempting to pin substantial VC forces into battle. Although taken by surprise, the Viet Cong retained the tactical initiative and once again avoided significant battle, leaving behind pockets of troops to engage the Americans in smaller battles of attrition. At the close of the operation, which had cost 450 VC dead against 83 allied losses, US and ARVN forces left the area, thinking it "pacified."

One month later four ARVN and 22 US battalions launched Operation Junction City, one of the largest operations of the entire war, into War Zone C in a renewed effort to destroy the 9th VC Division. Prior to the operation blocking forces took up positions along the Cambodian border to prevent a VC escape. On 22 February the main operation began with the 173rd Airborne participating in the only US combat parachute jump of the war. Along with landings by 249 helicopters US ground forces began the effort to envelop the Viet Cong. Though significant VC units were caught and responded by launching suicidal night attacks against American outposts, once again most VC forces made good their escape. During Junction City, which came to a halt on 14 May, nearly 3,000 Viet Cong died as compared to 282 allied fatalities. American troops exited the area believing they had destroyed the 9th Division, but they had not. Within a few months the 9th Division had made good its losses and returned to the area in preparation for the Tet Offensive. Giap did decide, though, to remove much of the VC infrastructure to safe havens in Cambodia on a permanent basis.

The nearly continuous fighting so close to Saigon did much damage to the South Vietnamese national infrastructure. Civilians were forcibly removed from their ancestral villages, vast areas were defoliated, and much of the area was declared a "free fire zone" meaning that devastating shelling could come at any time. Thus many civilians in this important area, along with others across the war-torn nation, became refugees. With their lives shattered and their future grim these refugees became a burden on the weak

South Vietnamese economy and also became possible new supporters of the Viet Cong. Despite the fact that US and ARVN forces were winning the "body count" battle, they were making little real headway in winning the war.

Throughout South Vietnam in 1967 US forces, operating in areas so geographically

Two US soldiers in the midst of a firefight during a Search and Destroy mission. Such missions and firefights were a common feature of the US strategy of attrition in 1967. (TRH Pictures)

center of VC support, the Mobile Riverine Force contested with the Viet Cong for control of the 3,000 square miles of waterways, rice paddies, and villages. These soldiers, usually arriving in battle in landing craft rather than helicopters, dealt severe blows to several Viet Cong units, including the 5th Nha Be Battalion and the 263rd Main Force Battalion. In one particularly savage encounter on 19 June near the village of Can Giuoc, 247 VC died in a single day. Even so the Viet Cong retained control of the tempo of the war and never lost control of their base areas, including the Cam San Secret Zone and the U-Minh Forest.

In the Central Highlands of Vietnam fighting raged in mountainous terrain covered in triple canopy rainforest. US forces of the 4th Division, based at Pleiku, squared off with NVA regulars of the 1st and 10th Divisions in a series of vicious, small-scale battles throughout the region. In November the fighting culminated in the Battle of Dak To when NVA forces laid siege to the Special Forces camp there. While attempting to raise the siege the 173rd Airborne Brigade discovered elements of the 174th NVA Regiment dug in on top of Hill 875. On 23 November, after five days of fighting that was reminiscent of the trench struggles of the First World War, US forces gained the top of Hill 875, only to discover that the enemy had fled. Within days US forces abandoned the hill and the Battle of Dak To had come to an end, leaving some 1,400 NVA and 289 Americans dead.

In the northern sector of South Vietnam along the DMZ, the fighting fell to the US Marines. To Westmoreland and MACV the area was critical, for it lay near the Ho Chi Minh Trail complex in Laos and sat astride the most likely route of NVA invasion of the South. In an attempt to defend the area and interdict Viet Cong supplies the Marines constructed defensive fortifications on a

diverse as almost to constitute separate wars, engaged in search and destroy missions and achieved similar results. In the heavily populated Mekong Delta south of Saigon, a

Soldiers of the Mobile Riverine Force charge out of their landing craft during 1967. Fighting in the wilderness of waterways that made up the Mekong Delta called for an unprecedented level of Army/Navy cooperation – rather than more typical tactics of airmobility. (TRH Pictures)

series of hilltops just south of the DMZ, dubbed the "McNamara Line." The westernmost base at Khe Sanh acted both as a defensive hub and a jumping-off point for covert missions against Viet Cong positions in Laos. To the east the forward firebase at Con Thien (the hill of angels) formed the lynchpin of the defensive line. To the communists the rather exposed positions of Khe Sanh and Con Thien presented inviting targets for attack. Unlike the areas further south, along the DMZ the communists would rely in the main on NVA regular forces, mainly the 325th Division and on fire support artillery based out of harm's way to the north of the DMZ.

During 1967 the fighting in the area of the DMZ was almost constant. At Khe Sanh NVA

forces attempted to surround the Marines, but in late April the 3rd Marines led a series of attacks on NVA positions in the hills surrounding the combat base, ending the immediate threat. Fighting was even stronger near Con Thien, where in September, augmented by a heavy artillery barrage, NVA forces launched a human wave attack, but were repulsed by murderous fire. From this point on the fighting at Con Thien settled down into a siege, in which 3,000 rounds of fire struck the Marine positions between 19 and 27 September. US forces responded with concentrated fire from artillery, battleships and B-52 bombers. In the carnage the NVA lost over 2,000 men and US forces lost 200, and both Khe Sanh and Con Thien remained in American hands.

A war of allies

Even while the United States fought its widely publicized war in Vietnam forces

The tunnel war

To defend themselves against withering American firepower Viet Cong insurgents throughout South Vietnam turned to the embrace of "mother earth." Using only the most rudimentary tools, and sometimes solely by hand, the insurgents created a vast network of tunnels that served as staging areas and defensive sanctuaries. In the Cu Chi area, only 25 miles north of Saigon, over 100 miles of tunnels connected nearly every village and hamlet and contained living quarters, hospitals and even armament factories. The tunnels were impervious to all but a direct hit by a B-52 bomber and were too narrow to allow entry to most Americans. In addition the tunnel entrances were so well hidden that the US 25th Division actually located its base camp directly on top of a major tunnel complex. Eventually US forces discovered the importance of the tunnel complexes and countered by sending lone warriors, dubbed "Tunnel Rats," to engage in a bitter, underground war. Armed only with pistols and flashlights the Tunnel Rats braved claustrophobia, booby traps and subterranean hand-to-hand fighting in an effort to oust the Viet Cong defenders. Eventually US forces resorted to brute force to overcome the tunnel threat, using massive bulldozers to scour the area and entomb the remaining Viet Cong inside their tunnel homes.

allied to the US struggled in greater anonymity. The military contributions of Thailand, Korea, Australia and New Zealand would have an important, but undervalued, impact on the war in Vietnam. As in the United States, though, the four allied nations would find that their roles in the conflict would become controversial – leading to lasting complications on their homefronts.

By 1968 Thailand, which was involved in fighting communist guerrillas along its own long border, devoted the Black Panther Division to the struggle in South Vietnam. Augmented by US advisors, the Thai force operated in III Corps tactical zone near Saigon. Supported by their own artillery in two firebases the Thais conducted several independent search and destroy operations aimed at denying supplies and sustenance to the Viet Cong. Though their area of operations was relatively quiet the Thais fought effectively, especially in their pacification efforts. Following 1971 Thai forces slowly withdrew from the conflict, eventually quitting the war in April 1972. Though the main conflict had ended the Thais would retain a keen interest as the regional war drew to a close in neighboring Laos and Cambodia.

South Korea, anxious both to oppose the spread of communism and to work closely with the United States, sent the largest allied force to Vietnam, reaching a high of 48,000 men in 1969. Hoping to avoid any comparisons with colonial control, Westmoreland urged the allied forces to work independently. The Korean force, which included elements of elite units such as the Capital (Tiger) Division and the 9th (White Horse) Division, operated mainly in II Corps tactical zone in and around Binh Dinh Province. Renowned for their anticommunist zeal and their brutality the Korean forces achieved great military success in their area of operations, but at a high price. Korean demands for funding from the United States led to a growing rift between the two allies, while Korean fighting methods would lead to bitter accusations of war crimes from Vietnam after the close of the conflict.

Australia began its commitment to the war in Vietnam quite early, sending the Australian Army Training Team Vietnam to the area in 1962 to train ARVN forces in jungle warfare. This elite unit, made up of soldiers from both Australia and New Zealand, remained in Vietnam until 1972 giving it one of the longest service records of the entire war. Though small, its motivated troops received over 100 decorations for bravery including four Victoria Crosses. As the conflict in Vietnam worsened Australia and New Zealand sent

The year of attrition

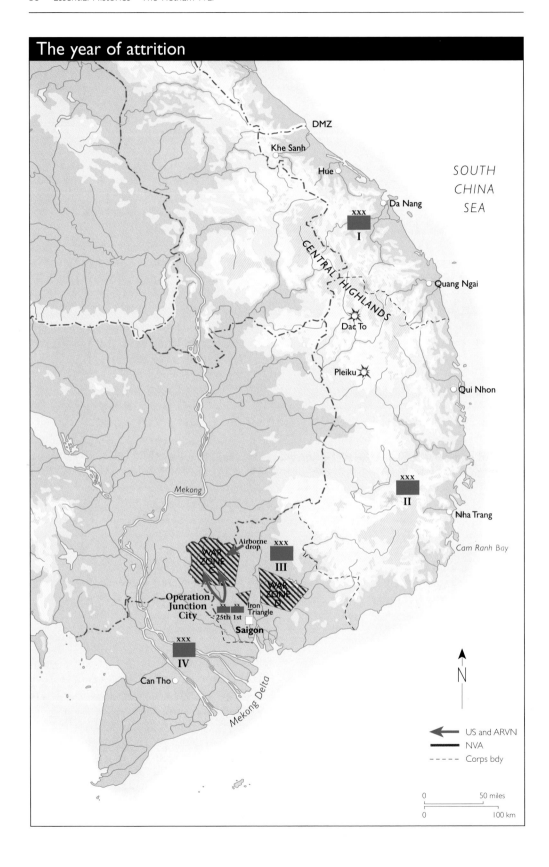

DMZ

Khe Sanh

Hue

Da Nang

SOUTH
CHINA
SEA

xxx
I

CENTRAL HIGHLANDS

Quang Ngai

Dac To

Pleiku

Qui Nhon

Mekong

xxx
II

Nha Trang

Cam Ranh Bay

Airborne
drop

WAR
ZONE
C

xxx
III

WAR
ZONE
D

Operation
Junction
City

xx   xx   Iron
25th 1st Triangle

Saigon

xxx
IV

Can Tho

Mekong Delta

N

US and ARVN
NVA
Corps bdy

0   50 miles
0   100 km

increasing numbers of troops – culminating in the arrival of the 1st Australian Task Force (ATF) in 1966. Based in Phuoc Tuy Province

LEFT Dividing South Vietnam into four corps zones of control, during 1967 US forces conducted a series of massive search and destroy missions in an effort to locate and destroy the strength of the NVA and the Viet Cong. Focal points of such missions included War Zone C, War Zone D and the Iron Triangle just north of Saigon. Operations in these areas, and in the Mekong Delta and the Central Highlands, though, failed to pin enemy units into decisive battle. Retaining the initiative the NVA and the VC would fight and then flee to their safe havens in Cambodia and Laos.

BELOW Fearing a cross-border invasion the US Marines constructed a series of defensive bases in the mountainous terrain south of the DMZ. From such bases as Con Thien and Khe Sanh, the marines would patrol the area – often in single companies. In some of the most bitter fighting of the conflict NVA regular divisions – often outnumbering the marines 5 to 1 – battled the marines for supremacy in the area. The fighting – sometimes on mountains over 3,000 feet in height – was nearly continuous and included several NVA sieges of the more vulnerable marine bases, including Khe Sanh. As a result of the bitter fighting the marines would suffer more casualties in Vietnam than they had in the Second World War.

the Australians specialized in counter-insurgency techniques designed to cut the Viet Cong off from their links to the population. In early 1966 a company of the 6th Royal Australian Regiment (RAR) clashed with a Viet Cong regiment near Xa Long Tan. In what was destined to be one of the biggest ATF battles of the war the 6th RAR lost 18 dead and 24 wounded while killing an estimated 245 VC. Though the ATF would fight other pitched battles, notably at Binh Ba in 1969, fighting on such a scale was not the norm. Constant patrolling and effective counterinsurgency techniques kept the VC under pressure and made Phuoc Tuy Province a model of pacification.

Though the ATF met with great success in Vietnam, the war as a whole caused great consternation on the Australian homefront. Strong initial pubic support for the Vietnam War began to wane in Australia, in part due to a controversial draft system. As in the United States once the war in Vietnam stagnated the draft in Australia became ever more divisive leading to political

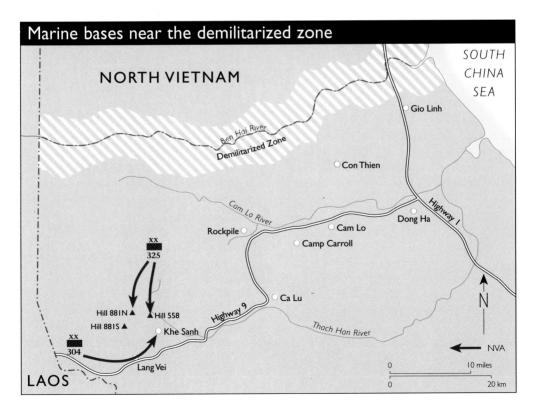

Marine bases near the demilitarized zone

SOUTH CHINA SEA

NORTH VIETNAM

Gio Linh

Ben Hai River

Demilitarized Zone

Con Thien

Cam Lo River

Highway 1

Dong Ha

Rockpile

Cam Lo

Camp Carroll

325

Ca Lu

N

Hill 881N

Hill 558

Highway 9

Thach Han River

Hill 881S

Khe Sanh

NVA

304

Lang Vei

0   10 miles

LAOS

0   20 km

turmoil and moratorium demonstrations across the country by 1970. The anti-Vietnam War movement in Australia understandably intersected with the other social and political issues of the era leading to ever-greater explosiveness. Over 50,000 Australians and New Zealanders would serve in the Vietnam War but like their American counterparts Australian veterans of the Vietnam War would return to a country divided.

The media in Vietnam

The role of the media during the Vietnam War remains controversial, and some historians suggest that a negative media image of the war in many ways caused the American defeat in Vietnam. As the war progressed televised coverage of the fighting in Vietnam became more and more important. Television journalists, most importantly Walter Cronkite, initially supported US actions in Vietnam. As the war played out every night in living rooms across the country, and ordinary Americans witnessed slaughter, views began to change, especially after the Tet Offensive. Images of the bloody Tet fighting, especially in Saigon, flooded American airwaves, including the infamous scene of South Vietnamese General Nguyen Ngoc Loan's summary execution of a VC prisoner. Cronkite, among others, felt that he had been duped by government assurances that the war in Vietnam was being won. He then announced on his evening news broadcast that the war in Vietnam had become a stalemate and that the US ought to seek a way out of the conflict, "not as victors but as an honorable people who lived up to their pledge to defend democracy and did the best they could." Nine million people viewed this broadcast, which marked the point at which middle America came to question the value of continuing the war in Vietnam.

The Tet Offensive

The Vietnam War had reached a critical turning point due both to the successes and failures of the attritional battles of 1967. Though they had been prepared for such a conflict, both Ho Chi Minh and Giap feared that the tremendous losses of 1967 would push their people to breaking point. Fearing ultimate defeat both men chose to eschew the strategy of protracted war in an effort to defeat US forces in a decisive battle. In their revolutionary ardor, though, the communists overlooked their military weaknesses, believing that a large-scale attack on US forces would lead to a general uprising that the Americans could not defeat. The strength of numbers would crush the illegitimate regime in Saigon and the American imperialists would come to realize that they could not win the war.

In the United States the slow progress of the war in Vietnam and numerous revelations about government dishonesty with regard to the conflict combined seriously to erode public support for the war. Anti-war protests grew in size and violence and garnered considerable media coverage. As a result the American electorate became increasingly polarized concerning the conflict – something that Johnson, who faced an imminent election, could not ignore. Believing the enemy to be nearly beaten Johnson called for a media blitz in favor of the administration's Vietnam policies. Accordingly, Westmoreland promised that the end of the war was in sight and that the enemy was so weakened as to be unable to launch any more major offensive actions. Westmoreland, however, was mistaken.

General Pham Hung developed the Tet Offensive as a three-phase plan. In preparation for this massive attack the Viet Cong had, in late 1967, lured US forces into the Vietnamese hinterlands, through a series of attacks and buildups, including the assault on Dak To and the concentration of forces around Khe Sanh. With American forces distant and distracted the Viet Cong began

Members of 4/173 Airborne Brigade move uphill into position as they prepare for the assault on Hill 875. (TRH/US Army)

the dangerous task of gathering together a force of 84,000 near the major cities of South Vietnam. By January of 1968 the Viet Cong buildup was complete, and the communists stood ready for their offensive – simultaneous assaults on all of the major cities of South Vietnam, guarded by inferior ARVN opponents. The urban attacks were timed to take place during a ceasefire in celebration of the Tet Lunar New Year. Giap hoped that surprise would lead to initial victories before American troops could react and that seizure of only a few cities would result in the general uprising that would win the war.

Early on the morning of 30 January 1968 Viet Cong and NVA forces launched the Tet Offensive. The main focal point of the attack was Saigon, involving 35 battalions under the command of General Tran Van Tra. Communist forces did not attack in an organized effort to overthrow Saigon, rather they chose to strike out at targets of political and military importance in an effort to paralyze government control of the city and spur the hoped for general uprising. Toward this end specialist units struck at the Presidential Palace, the radio station and both the MACV and the ARVN headquarters. Most importantly, though, 19 men from the Viet Cong C-10 Sapper Battalion attacked the US embassy compound, prompting a six-hour battle with US military police. The Viet Cong sappers all perished without penetrating the embassy proper. However, the US media covered the attack extensively. Though the attack had failed, communist forces had penetrated to the very heart of American power in South Vietnam, indicating that the war there was much more serious than expected and that US boasts of imminent victory were misguided at best, and calculated lies at worst.

Across Saigon the Viet Cong used surprise to make initial gains, but failed in their overall objectives due to a quick reaction by powerful US and ARVN forces. Fighting was especially strong at the critical Tan Son Nhut airbase. Three VC battalions struck the facility surprising the American defenders and resulting in a hand-to-hand struggle that raged across the airfield and many of its buildings. With the aid of a relief column from the 25th Infantry based near Cu Chi the defenders eventually repulsed the VC attack with heavy losses. It was the same across most of the city; exposed VC forces

LEFT A tunnel rat makes ready to take the war to the VC amidst an underground war. (TRH Pictures)

BELOW Representatives of American news media interview US soldiers during action in South Vietnam. The continuous media coverage created the first "Television War" and did much to dampen American enthusiasm for the conflict. (TRH Pictures)

were massacred at the hands of US and ARVN firepower, and the offensive collapsed in a matter of days. Even more important, though, the population had failed to rise up in support of the communists. It seemed that the great Tet gamble had failed.

The Tet Offensive as a whole followed a similar ebb and flow to the fighting in Saigon, except in the city of Hue. The home of the old imperial capital, Hue is divided into two sections by the Perfume River. The new city is south of the river, while north of the river lies the walled Citadel. On 31 January nearly 8,000 men of the 4th and 6th NVA regiments invaded Hue and quickly seized most of the Citadel and much of the new city as well. In the northern corner of the Citadel remnants of the 1st ARVN Division held out, and in the new city some 200 Americans and Australians held firm in the MACV compound. Demonstrating its surprise the Marine command at Phu Bai, only a few miles to the south, initially sent a single company to restore the situation. As the scale of the disaster dawned on the Americans, though, more and more troops were dedicated to the battle in Hue and in an effort to cut off communist supply lines to the city.

At first US and ARVN forces made scant progress against an enemy who had finally chosen to stand and fight, though they had relieved the beleaguered defenders of the MACV compound. Fighting in the winding, narrow confines of Hue's streets negated the allied edges in mobility and firepower. It was not until 11 February, when the ARVN gave the go ahead for the use of heavy weaponry in the city that significant progress began to be made. By 9 February US Marines had cleared most of the new city, but the fighting in the Citadel, handled mainly by the ARVN, raged on, in many ways resembling the fighting in Stalingrad in the Second World War, as soldiers fought hand-to-hand for every square foot amid the rubble. The fighting for the Citadel raged until 24 February when ARVN Major Pham Van Dinh once again hoisted the South Vietnamese flag signifying victory.

During the struggle in Hue the communists had been able to implement their societal revolution unchecked for nearly an entire month. Terror ruled as VC and NVA soldiers combed the residential districts for supporters of the South Vietnamese regime. Estimates vary but communist forces rounded up and killed between 3,000 and 6,000 civilians. In the fighting across the city many more perished: US forces lost 216 dead, ARVN forces lost 384, NVA and VC forces lost 5,000. More than 1,000 civilians perished in the fighting and over 50 percent of the city was destroyed, leaving 116,000 homeless people from a total population of only 140,000. The civilian losses at the hands of the communists held even greater significance, foreshadowing the consequences of a communist victory. If US forces exited South Vietnam too quickly it seemed that the communists would unleash a societal holocaust upon supporters of the South Vietnamese regime, possibly slaughtering millions.

The final stage of Giap's plan for the Tet Offensive involved an attack on the American Marine base at Khe Sanh after gathering some 40,000 troops to oppose the 6,000 marines that defended Khe Sanh and four surrounding hills. Westmoreland had expected such an attack and was ready when on 20 January the siege of Khe Sanh began. Giap hoped that his forces, which had cut off ground communication with Khe Sanh, could cripple the airstrip there and that artillery fire could pound the Marines into submission. In addition NVA forces launched infantry attacks on more isolated US outposts and eventually seized Hill 861 and Lang Vei Special Forces Camp. As the noose tightened around the beleaguered Marines, Westmoreland launched a planned counterstrike and unleashed Operation Niagara against the concentrated NVA forces. American fighter-bombers and B-52s struck communist positions around the clock. During a period of the most concentrated bombing in the history of warfare US air forces dropped bomb tonnage equivalent to 10 Hiroshima-sized atomic bombs.

At the end of February, heralded by their heaviest artillery barrage of the war, the

304th NVA Regiment launched a human wave assault on Khe Sanh, but it was obliterated by heavy US firepower. Though the outcome was no longer in doubt fighting continued at Khe Sanh until 8 April, when the arrival of ground units lifted the 77-day siege. Giap was denied his great victory as the Marines had held out against heavy odds, supplied by air from an airstrip that remained operational for the entire length of the siege. US and ARVN forces lost some 400 dead during the siege, but the constant pounding of Operation Niagara had inflicted an estimated 12,000 dead upon the communist forces, making the siege of Khe Sanh a resounding victory for American force of arms.

The Tet Offensive and its attendant attack on Khe Sanh had been a total failure for the communists. Of the 84,000 troops committed to Tet, nearly 58,000 had been killed, almost wiping out the Viet Cong as an effective fighting force. The scale of the disaster compelled the remaining VC cadres to retreat into the Vietnamese hinterlands to regroup, in the process abandoning land that had been under Viet Cong control for years. From this point, due to the demise of the Viet Cong the war became more conventional, and was controlled more directly from Hanoi. Also the Communists had expected that the ARVN would crumble, but it had fought hard and well, indicating that South Vietnam was coming of age and was something more than a lackey state of the US. Tet had been an ill-advised, demoralizing, controversial, comprehensive defeat but surprisingly it would also turn the tide of the war in favor of the communists.

American and South Vietnamese armed forces had achieved a great tactical victory in the Tet Offensive, and both Westmoreland and Johnson sensed that the war was nearing an end. Hoping that continued pressure would seal an inevitable victory Westmoreland longed to pursue reeling enemy forces into their hiding places in a massive offensive push. General Earle Wheeler, the Chairman of the Joint Chiefs of Staff, believed that the continuing Vietnam War had seriously weakened US force levels throughout the world. As a result Westmoreland and Wheeler agreed to request a call-up of an additional 206,000 troops, both to achieve the final victory in Vietnam and redress US neglect of its ground forces in Europe.

The request for additional troops caught Johnson and his top civilian advisors unawares. McNamara, in many ways the architect of US policy in Vietnam, who was leaving the administration partly because he had already come to the conclusion that the war there was misguided, advised Johnson to reject the troop request. Several factors added to Johnson's indecision. The scale of the proposed troop deployment would necessitate a call-up of National Guard forces, requiring a more standard military mobilization and a national call to war. Johnson realized that such a move would threaten American economic prosperity and the future of his Great Society.

The final problem faced by the administration was one of perception. The surprise and ferocity of the Tet Offensive were shocking to many, and the fact that enemy forces had penetrated so easily to the center of US control on South Vietnam was equally disturbing. Though Westmoreland characterized Tet as a great attritional victory the nature of such a victory was difficult for those not directly involved in the conflict to understand. US forces had seized no major enemy territory and the only sign of victory was the high "body count." It seemed, though, that the communist forces in Vietnam had a nearly limitless supply of manpower. Tet proved to many that the US government was lying to its own people regarding the nature of the war, continuing a trail of prevarication that some traced back to the Gulf of Tonkin Resolution. Instead of presaging victory, Tet indicated that the war in Vietnam would become more serious and require greater sacrifice of lives and wealth.

American involvement in the Vietnam War had reached its climax. As American support for the conflict began to unravel in a stunning series of protests and civil disobedience, Johnson had to decide

The Tet Offensive

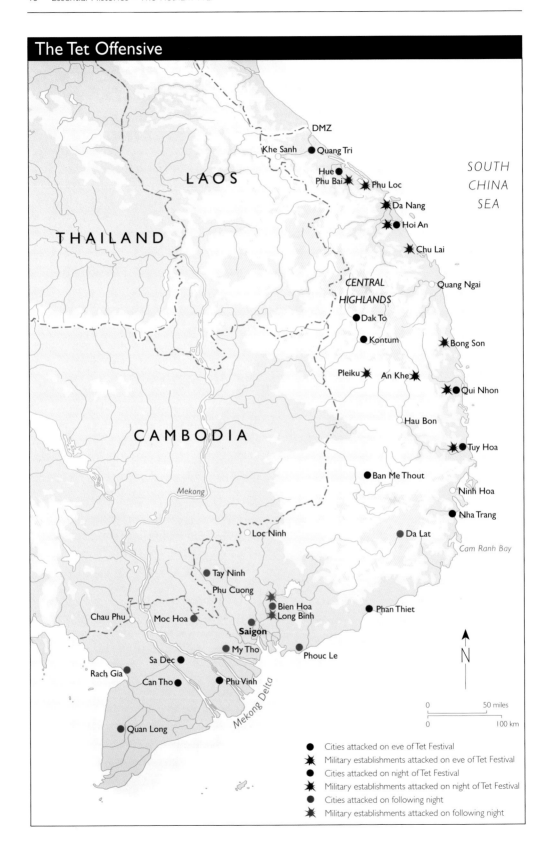

DMZ

Khe Sanh   ● Quang Tri

Hue ●
Phu Bai ✳   ✳ Phu Loc

✳ Da Nang
✳● Hoi An

✳ Chu Lai

*SOUTH
CHINA
SEA*

*CENTRAL
HIGHLANDS*

LAOS

THAILAND

Quang Ngai

● Dak To

● Kontum   ✳ Bong Son

Pleiku ✳   An Khe ✳   ✳● Qui Nhon

○ Hau Bon

CAMBODIA   ✳ Tuy Hoa

● Ban Me Thout

Mekong   ○ Ninh Hoa

● Nha Trang

○ Loc Ninh   ● Da Lat

Cam Ranh Bay

● Tay Ninh

Phu Cuong

Chau Phu ○   Moc Hoa ●   ✳ Bien Hoa
                ✳ Long Binh   ● Phan Thiet

Saigon ●

● My Tho
Sa Dec ●   Phouc Le ●
Rach Gia ●
        Can Tho ●   ● Phu Vinh

Mekong Delta

● Quan Long

N

0 ————————— 50 miles
0 ————————— 100 km

●   Cities attacked on eve of Tet Festival
✳   Military establishments attacked on eve of Tet Festival
●   Cities attacked on night of Tet Festival
✳   Military establishments attacked on night of Tet Festival
●   Cities attacked on following night
✳   Military establishments attacked on following night

The attack on Hue, 31 January 1968

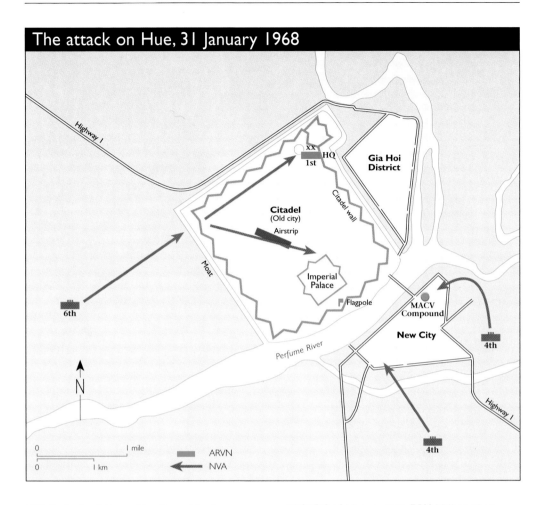

LEFT During the Tet Lunar New Year celebrations over 80,000 Viet Cong and NVA soldiers struck most of the urban areas across South Vietnam in a surprise attack, hoping that their actions would spark a nationwide revolution. Though they had achieved considerable surprise and wreaked havoc in urban areas – especially Saigon and Hue – the Tet Offensive failed, leading to overwhelming casualties. Another aspect of the Tet Offensive – attacks upon US military bases – most notably Khe Sanh and Cam Ranh Bay – also failed in its objective. The Tet Offensive was a comprehensive military defeat for communist forces, nearly destroying the VC. However, the Tet Offensive also marked a turning point in American attitudes toward the Vietnam War.

ABOVE On 31 January some 7,500 NVA attackers swept into the old imperial capital of Hue from all sides – overwhelming most of the ARVN defenders and taking control of the city. Caught off guard the ARVN and US marines quickly counterattacked, leading to over a month of bloody, urban fighting. While the NVA instituted a societal purge the US marines recaptured the New City south of the Perfume River, while the ARVN reclaimed the ancient Citadel north of the river. During the vicious struggle over 10,000 people perished, including between 3,000 and 6,000 civilians.

whether or not to approve the troop requests and transform Vietnam into a true war. For advice in the critical decision Johnson turned to Clark Clifford, the new Secretary of Defense. Taking his mandate very seriously Clifford set out to study American policy in Vietnam in a systematic way. He and a

special task force were stunned when they discovered that the United States had a frightening lack of understanding regarding the Vietnam War:

I could not find out when the war was going to end: I could not find out the manner in which it was going to end. I could not find out whether the new requests for men and equipment were

LEFT During the struggle for Khe Sanh US Marines struggle forward toward the summit of Hill 881. (Corbis)

going to be enough, or whether it would take more and, if more, how much … All I had was the statement, given with too little self-assurance to be comforting, that if we persisted for an indeterminate length of time, the enemy would choose not to go on.

Based on his findings Clifford not only decided to advise Johnson to reject the troop requests, but also that the United States should exit the conflict entirely. The election of 1968 only added to the confusion. Sensing weakness both Eugene McCarthy and Robert Kennedy chose to run against Johnson for the Democratic nomination for president on a platform of peace in Vietnam. With the Great Society in tatters, and his presidency in doubt Johnson had to face the fact that his policy in Vietnam had been misguided. On 31 March a crushed and beaten Johnson delivered one of the most stunning televised speeches in American history. He informed the American people of the halt of Operation Rolling Thunder and that the US military would begin a gradual withdrawal from Vietnam, as much as admitting that the war there had been lost. He ended his speech with a bombshell about which only he and his speechwriter were aware:

With America's sons in fields far away, with America's future under challenge right here at home … I do not believe that I should devote an hour or a day of my time to any personal partisan causes … Accordingly, I shall not seek, and I will not accept the nomination of my party for another term as your president.

The aftermath of the Tet Offensive had significantly altered the nature of the war in Vietnam. The great victory had been seen as a defeat in the United States, leading to the demise of Johnson's presidency, ironically making him a casualty of his own misguided war. The slow process that led to the end of the Vietnam War had begun.

A changing war

As protests erupted on American streets and peace talks opened in Paris, Westmoreland sought to crush weakened VC and NVA resistance in South Vietnam. North of Saigon US and ARVN forces launched Operation Toan Thang (Complete Victory) in an effort to eradicate enemy strongholds in War Zones C and D. In the largest search and destroy operation of the entire Vietnam War some 80 US and ARVN battalions swept through the area, but once again failed to destroy the remaining enemy forces before they could flee to their Cambodian sanctuaries. Not only had allied troops failed to destroy communist forces, they even failed in their effort to secure Saigon – for in May the Viet Cong launched a series of "Mini-Tet" attacks throughout the city.

In the Central Highlands US forces launched Operation Delaware – an air mobile assault on VC and NVA staging areas in the A Shau Valley – designed to end the continuing threat of further enemy attacks on Hue. Covered in jungle and surrounded by 3,000-foot mountains, the A Shau was a forbidding target. On 19 April troopers of the 7th Cavalry hit the northern end of the valley – but were greeted with withering anti-aircraft fire and lost 10 helicopters. As they had further south the VC and NVA abandoned their bases in the A Shau, leaving behind a rearguard to resist in an area dubbed "the Punchbowl." During Operation Delaware US forces captured and destroyed large quantities of enemy supplies before exiting the A Shau Valley in August. Shortly thereafter the NVA returned and rebuilt their base areas, necessitating a further US effort against the area in 1969. Further north along the DMZ fighting remained heavy especially near the village of Dai Do. Quickly, though, the struggle along the DMZ settled down into an uncomfortable stalemate for the remainder of the year, one involving sieges, counter-sieges and almost continuous casualties on both sides.

On 3 July 1968 General Creighton Abrams succeeded Westmoreland in command of US forces in South Vietnam. Sensitive to the need to work within the framework of crumbling American support for the Vietnam War, Abrams changed the conduct of the conflict in several fundamental ways. Aiming at greater tactical flexibility Abrams abandoned the policies of search and destroy and attrition and informed Johnson that, "We've got to go beyond smashing up the enemy's main-force units. We have to do that selectively, but the way to get off the treadmill is to get after his infrastructure and guerrillas." Thus Abrams chose to fight the Vietnam War in a much less traditional way and initiated his "One War" strategy, designed to blend traditional military efforts with increased attempts at pacification throughout the South Vietnamese countryside. Toward this end Abrams limited multi-battalion search and destroy missions that left the tactical initiative in the hands of the enemy in favor of small unit patrols and ambushes designed to

General Creighton Abrams – Westmoreland's successor and architect of the "One War" strategy. (Corbis)

provide security for the villages of South Vietnam. Thus US combat missions under Abrams would be much smaller, and were designed to cut the enemy off from his civilian support in South Vietnam.

Abrams also placed renewed emphasis on less traditional aspects of his counter insurgency campaign. Civilian Operations and Revolutionary Development Support (CORDS) played a major role in the One War strategy by working for economic development on the village level and through training and equipping village self-defense forces. Aided by the Central Intelligence Agency (CIA), Abrams also lashed out at the VC infrastructure in South Vietnam. In villages across the nation VC functionaries worked rather openly to collect taxes and procure supplies and recruits from the people. A destruction of that infrastructure would deny the VC the wherewithal for effective operations. The controversial Phoenix Program became the cornerstone of the US and ARVN effort to eradicate the VC infrastructure and met with significant success – capturing 34,000 VC operatives and "neutralizing" thousands more.

Vietnamization

In the wake of Johnson's decision not to run for president, the Democratic Party fell into turmoil, which culminated in rioting at the Democratic National Convention in Chicago. Richard Nixon, the Republican nominee who promised to end the war in Vietnam, won a narrow victory in the election and in 1969 took office and control of the Vietnam War. Nixon, and his chief advisor, Secretary of State Henry Kissinger, initiated a heavy bombing campaign of communist bases in Cambodia, code-named the MENU Series. However, the communists held firm and continued to prolong the conflict hoping that public opinion would force the US to abandon South Vietnam. With only limited military options, and faced with a recalcitrant enemy Nixon and

Secretary of State Henry Kissinger and President Richard Nixon – who, after attempts to alter the nature of the conflict, would preside over American withdrawal from Vietnam. (Topham Picturepoint)

Kissinger slowly developed their policy of "Vietnamization." The plan called for a slow, phased withdrawal of US forces from the war while US aid and training would convert the ARVN into a force capable of defending South Vietnam. In addition the Nixon administration planned to take the diplomatic offensive through a rapprochement with China and the Soviet Union, aimed partly at cutting their support for the North Vietnamese war effort. The first act of Vietnamization took place in June 1969 when Nixon ordered the reduction of the troop ceiling in Vietnam by 25,000 men.

In the spring of 1969 US intelligence detected a renewed enemy buildup in the A Shau Valley. As a result, on 10 May allied forces began a search and destroy mission in the area and discovered an NVA force dug in on Hill 937, later known as "Hamburger Hill." After an intense artillery barrage on 13 May elements of the 187th Infantry assaulted the hill but were repulsed by heavy defensive fire. The fighting continued for days amid torrential rain and constant shelling that transformed the battlefield into a sea of mud and shattered trees. Finally, after nearly a week of constant fighting, three US and one ARVN battalion assaulted the NVA defensive emplacements and finally reached the summit of Hamburger Hill, only to find that the enemy had fled in the night. US forces had suffered 56 dead and had inflicted an estimated 700 fatalities on the defenders. After the attritional victory US forces exited the A Shau Valley. The assault on Hamburger Hill received massive press coverage, and caused widespread protest, the vehemence of which convinced Nixon to tell Abrams to hold down US casualties in Vietnam, making Hamburger Hill one of the last attritional battles of the Vietnam War.

Into Cambodia

As Vietnamization proceeded apace the situation in Southeast Asia abruptly changed for the worse. Under the rule of Prince Noradoom Sihanouk Cambodia had long walked a tightrope of neutrality in the Vietnam War. The crafty leader had kept his nation from the worst ravages of war by allowing the communists to utilize Cambodian border areas with impunity and also by turning a blind eye to allied incursions into the area. However, in March 1970 pro-American General Lon Nol overthrew Sihanouk and ordered the North Vietnamese out of Cambodia. Unwilling to sacrifice their safe havens and logistic support areas, the North Vietnamese made common cause with the communist Khmer Rouge insurgents of Cambodia to destroy the Lon Nol government.

Cambodian forces quickly lost ground to the communist offensive, which enjoyed the support of the popular Sihanouk. Alarmed by the threat to Phnom Penh, Nixon agreed to support a major cross-border invasion of Cambodia designed to save the Lon Nol regime. Such an operation, long supported by US military leaders, at best would destroy the communist forces in the area. Even if only moderately successful the Cambodian invasion would disrupt the communist logistic support system, buying valuable time for the success of Vietnamization. Though Nixon realized that the operation was constitutionally questionable and would cause a firestorm of protest in America he deemed the risk worthwhile.

On 29 April, after only a short period of planning, an ARVN invasion of the strategic "Parrot's Beak" section of Cambodia began a series of operations that would involve 50,000 ARVN and 30,000 American troops. US and ARVN troops followed with an invasion of the "Fishhook" region of Cambodia while further south Riverine forces cut communist logistic ties to the critical port of Sihanoukville as part of the SEALORDS Program. Across Cambodia communist rearguards fought bitter struggles against superior allied firepower enabling most of the main force NVA units to slip away. Fearing a political backlash Nixon had placed important limitations on the Cambodian Incursion, which meant that US forces could penetrate no more than 19 miles into Cambodia and had to exit the nation by 30 June.

Though ARVN forces were less restricted such limitations kept allied forces from achieving decisive victory. Over 11,000 communists were killed in the invasion and Lon Nol's government received a temporary reprieve, but the majority of NVA and Khmer Rouge forces were able to make good their escape to new safe havens. Allied actions had destroyed much of the communist logistic network but, following the pattern set in Vietnam, communist forces would return and rebuild after US and ARVN forces left Cambodia. The allied victory in the Cambodian Incursion was flawed at best, and was representative of the Vietnam War as a whole. Political pressures within the United States had forced limitations on the operation that made meaningful victory impossible. Such limitations were little regarded on the US home front, where the Cambodian Incursion was met with a wave of protest culminating in violence that claimed the lives of six students at Kent State and Jackson State universities.

The successes of the Cambodian Incursion forced the North Vietnamese to become more reliant upon the Laotian sector of the Ho Chi Minh Trail, a development carefully monitored by allied intelligence. Realizing that US support for the Vietnam War was fast fading South Vietnamese President Thieu pressed for a preemptive strike against the communist buildup in Laos. The plan received support from Abrams, but the invasion of Laos, dubbed Operation Lam Son 719, would mainly be an ARVN affair. The plan called for 15,000 ARVN troops to advance to Tchepone in Laos, disrupting the communist logistic network. However, Giap and the NVA were expecting such an attack. Deeming the area too important to surrender Giap gathered nearly 40,000 troops and

A South Vietnamese soldier arrests Viet Cong fighters near a bunker during Operation Lam Son 719. Though the ARVN initially made great gains – they soon succumbed to an unexpectedly ferocious North Vietnamese counterattack. (TRH Pictures)

made ready to stand and fight for the first time since the Tet Offensive.

On 8 February 1971 ARVN troops of the 1st Armored Brigade and the Airborne Division, under the command of General Hoang Xuan Lam, began to advance down Route 9 into Laos. The attack quickly lost momentum as three NVA divisions supported by T-34 and T-54/55 tanks offered stiff resistance. Pressured on his exposed flanks General Lam chose to assault Tchepone using air mobile tactics, and the city fell on 6 March due in large part to "clandestine" US air support. Though the advance had been successful, the ARVN

forces now found themselves in a very exposed position as NVA forces massed on their flanks. Sensing impending disaster, on 10 March Lam ordered a retreat back to South Vietnam, but it was too late. Harried by unrelenting NVA attacks the ARVN retreat quickly became a rout. US air power came to the aid of the retreating ARVN, flying over 90,000 sorties but was limited by heavy antiaircraft fire and bad weather. Only the heroic efforts of US helicopter pilots and the 101st Airborne Division kept disaster at bay. In the end only one half of the ARVN invasion force returned to South Vietnam, and 108 US helicopters were lost. Though Nixon trumpeted Lam Son 719 as a great victory, and the communist logistic network had received another shock, the results of the invasion of Laos did not bode well for Vietnamization. In the main, though the ARVN had fought hard it remained poorly

The Cambodian incursion and Operation Lam Son 719

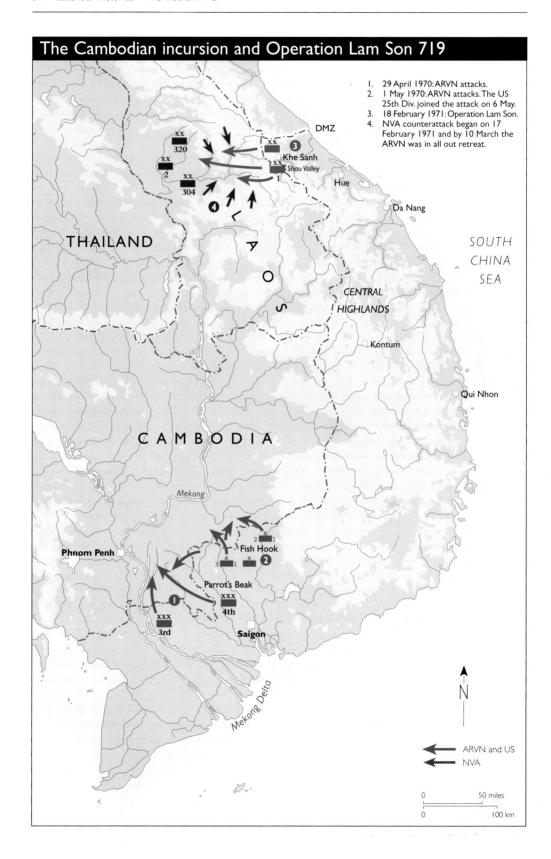

1. 29 April 1970: ARVN attacks.
2. 1 May 1970: ARVN attacks. The US 25th Div. joined the attack on 6 May.
3. 18 February 1971: Operation Lam Son.
4. NVA counterattack began on 17 February 1971 and by 10 March the ARVN was in all out retreat.

DMZ

THAILAND

LAOS

SOUTH CHINA SEA

CENTRAL HIGHLANDS

Kontum

Qui Nhon

CAMBODIA

Mekong

Phnom Penh

Fish Hook

Parrot's Beak

Saigon

Mekong Delta

N

ARVN and US
NVA

0   50 miles
0   100 km

In an effort to win decisive victories over the NVA and to aid the process of Vietnamization US and ARVN forces undertook two major offensives against NVA staging areas in Cambodia and Laos. Beginning in late April 1970 US and ARVN forces struck the Parrot's Beak and Fishhook regions of Cambodia. Though the NVA fled the attacks did much to disrupt their logistic support network in the region. In February 1971 ARVN forces tried to repeat the success by striking into Laos. Here, though, the NVA chose to stand and fight – transforming a seemingly successful ARVN attack into a bloody rout. Though some ARVN units had fought well – the overall South Vietnamese performance in 1970 and 1971 gave little hope for the future.

commanded – the servant of a government that did little to earn the support of its own people.

The remainder of 1971 saw relative calm on the battlefields and on the US home front. American forces continued to withdraw, retaining only 140,000 troops in the country at year's end. The fighting dwindled to small unit affairs as both sides conserved their strength. The relative military inactivity also kept the war a political non-issue on the streets of America. The US public had tired of the war and of political tension and yearned for normalcy. At the same time there were advances in the Paris Peace Talks where Kissinger and North Vietnamese representative Le Duc Tho edged nearer to a cease-fire agreement as both men realized that a US withdrawal from the conflict was fast becoming reality. On the international front Nixon kept the pressure on North Vietnam through the process of détente with China and the Soviet Union. Impending presidential visits to both Beijing and Moscow greatly worried the North Vietnamese. Giap, whose power had risen since the death of Ho Chi Minh in 1969, thought that the Soviets and Chinese might abandon Vietnam as they had in 1954, causing a political defeat when military victory over the United States seemed so close at hand.

In 1971 the Communist Party Plenum decided to launch a massive, conventional offensive against South Vietnam in an effort to seek a decisive military victory and end the war. Few US combat forces remained and the ARVN seemed weak and incompetent. Immediate victory would also preempt any long-term influence of détente on the outcome of the conflict. General Giap committed 12 divisions totaling some 150,000 men to the coming Nguyen Hue Offensive. The plan called for a three-pronged attack: an offensive from the DMZ aimed at the seizure of Hue, an offensive in the Central Highlands aimed at Kontum, and an attack from Cambodia aimed at Saigon.

On 30 March 30,000 NVA soldiers, supported by tanks and artillery, crossed the DMZ and slammed into the vastly outnumbered ARVN defenders of Quang Tri Province. ARVN forces crumbled before the massive assault, eventually losing a bitter struggle for Quang Tri City. Stiffened by reinforcements and inspired by a new commander, General Ngo Quang Troung, in May the outnumbered ARVN held fast at Hue in the face of concerted NVA assaults. Aided by massive amounts of US air support the ARVN counterattacked in June and reclaimed Quang Tri City in savage street fighting in September.

In the Central Highlands two NVA divisions quickly seized Dak To and drove on to the pivotal town of Kontum. Though the defenders fought valiantly it was round-the-clock airstrikes from US B-52s that broke the back of the NVA assault and by mid-May Kontum had been saved. Further south NVA forces advanced against sporadic ARVN resistance to the critical road junction town of An Loc. Street fighting raged in An Loc for weeks as US air power obliterated entire NVA units. The Nguyen Hue Offensive, dubbed the Easter Offensive in America, had failed. Used to fighting a guerrilla war the NVA had proven less than proficient in conventional war, especially in the areas of command and control. The ARVN had fought doggedly with its back against the wall, indicating that the South Vietnamese fighting man was capable of great success when properly led and motivated. However, the decisive factor in the failure of the Nguyen Hue Offensive had been American air

Three American B-52s pound enemy targets. It was the strength of the B-52s during Operations Linebacker I and II that did much to bring the North Vietnamese to an eventual peace agreement. (TRH Pictures)

power. Caught in the open NVA units proved vulnerable to aerial assault, losing over 100,000 men. Such a rate of loss was simply unacceptable to the North Vietnamese and caused them finally to seek a true end to American involvement in the Vietnam War through negotiation.

As the Easter Offensive raged Nixon decided to unleash the power of the US Airforce on North Vietnam in Operation Linebacker. Involving the strength of 210 B-52s – representing one half of the US Strategic Air Command bomber fleet – Linebacker unleashed even heavier bombing than Operation Rolling Thunder had done. Unlike Rolling Thunder, Linebacker targeted both Hanoi and Haiphong in an effort to drive North Vietnam to an acceptance of the American definition of peace with honor.

Aided by the first use of "smart bombs" and the mining of Haiphong Harbor, Operation Linebacker flattened most of North Vietnam's war industry and severely disrupted the inward flow of military supplies from China and the Soviet Union. The bombing raged for six months as the Easter Offensive ground to a halt. Battered and fearing total abandonment by their allies the North Vietnamese returned to the abandoned peace talks in Paris.

By now both the United States and North Vietnam simply wanted an end to US involvement in the Vietnam War. Nixon and Kissinger both realized that the war would continue after a US withdrawal. Both men also realized that South Vietnam could not survive alone. Nevertheless, American involvement in the conflict had to come to an end. Toward this end US negotiators agreed to allow communist military forces to remain in place in South Vietnam and also agreed to allow the communists a place in the political system. In effect America agreed to leave the situation in South Vietnam

Representatives of the US, North Vietnam, South Vietnam, and the Viet Cong sign the cease-fire accord in Paris on 27 January 1973. The war in Vietnam, though, would continue without direct American involvement. (TRH Pictures)

much as it had found it in 1965. For their part the North Vietnamese agreed to allow the Thieu government to remain in place with US support, a concession that was anathema to the communists since it provided the South Vietnamese government with a measure of legitimacy.

On 8 October 1972 the two sides reached agreement in Paris in negotiations that had not included the South Vietnamese. This omission clearly indicated that the negotiations were not concerned with the continued existence of South Vietnam, but with an American exit from a conflict that had cost so much. For his part President Thieu realized that the proposed peace agreement represented a death sentence for his country and refused to sign. The peace talks stalled yet again. After a safe victory in the presidential election of 1972 Nixon felt more able to stand up to his recalcitrant ally but had to force the North Vietnamese

back to the bargaining table. Thus on 18 December Nixon unleashed Operation Linebacker II. This controversial and costly bombing campaign proved effective and on 8 January 1973 all sides signed the Paris Peace Accords ending US involvement in the Vietnam War. Within 60 days all US troops were to exit South Vietnam and the North Vietnamese were to return all US prisoners of war. For the United States the war in Vietnam was over. That the United States made its exit from the Vietnam War without resolving the political questions that had started the conflict guaranteed that the war would continue.

FOLLOWING PAGE Amid a seemingly successful peace process on 30 March 1972 NVA units launched their largest offensive to date — a three-phase campaign aimed at the overthrow of South Vietnam. Surprised and suffering great losses ARVN forces initially fell back, losing important ground — most notably Quang Tri City. However, after initial defeats the ARVN held firm — with massive US air support — at Hue and at Kontum. It was at An Loc, though, where the fighting was the most bitter as the ARVN and the NVA engaged in hand-to-hand urban warfare for weeks. In the end the Easter Offensive was a failure — held up by ARVN resistance and destroyed by US airpower — helping force North Vietnam to opt for a compromise peace.

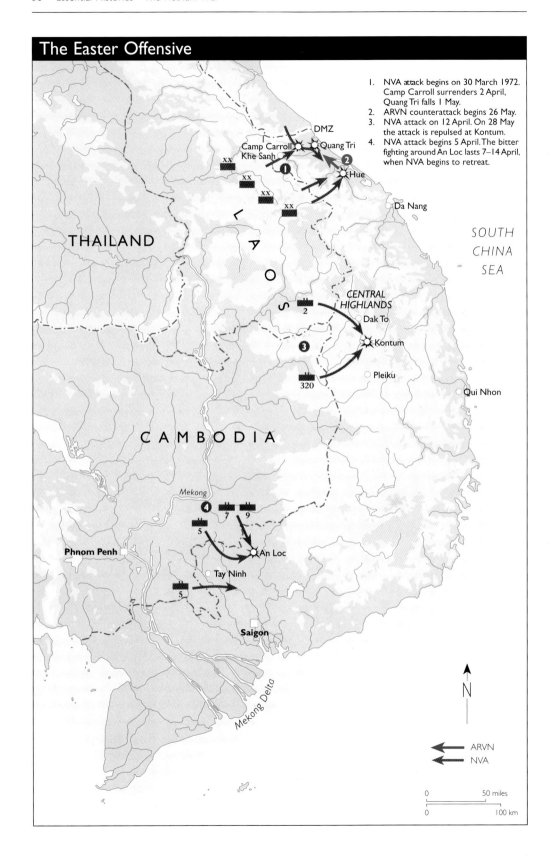

The Easter Offensive

1. NVA attack begins on 30 March 1972.
   Camp Carroll surrenders 2 April,
   Quang Tri falls 1 May.
2. ARVN counterattack begins 26 May.
3. NVA attack on 12 April. On 28 May
   the attack is repulsed at Kontum.
4. NVA attack begins 5 April. The bitter
   fighting around An Loc lasts 7–14 April,
   when NVA begins to retreat.

DMZ

Camp Carroll
Khe Sanh
Quang Tri

Hue

Da Nang

THAILAND

L A O S

SOUTH
CHINA
SEA

CENTRAL
HIGHLANDS

Dak To

2

3

Kontum

Pleiku

320

Qui Nhon

C A M B O D I A

Mekong

4

7   9

5

An Loc

Phnom Penh

Tay Ninh

5

Saigon

Mekong Delta

N

ARVN

NVA

0   50 miles

0   100 km

John Young

In mid-May 1966 I was near the end of my third year of college at the University of Minnesota. Exactly one year later I was an infantry squad leader in Vietnam. The year in between was the last year that I was young.

Of course it was a different world then. Certainly it was a different United States.

The Cold War put an edge on life, but we were a confident people, with no reason to doubt that we could deal with whatever the world might send us.

Staff Sergeant John Winston Young at age 21 during 1967. (John Young)

Looking back, it is hard to believe that we were once so innocent. For 190 years the United States had built on an almost unbroken record of success, and the little war in Southeast Asia that we seemed to have stumbled into was surely no cause to fear for our future. Quite the contrary: my father and all his brothers, and all of my mother's brothers had served in World War II, and Vietnam was simply my generation's call to duty. I honestly wanted to serve. There was not the least doubt in my mind that what the US was doing in Vietnam was right. The US was always right, and this was a challenge that John Kennedy might have had in mind when he spoke of, "supporting any friend," and "opposing any foe," and "bearing any burden" in defense of liberty.

It was all so simple, and so generous. South Vietnam was a small country that wanted to stay free, and its communist northern neighbor was trying to conquer it. The South Vietnamese had asked the US for help, and we were helping. It was a little like the Peace Corps with rifles. The enemy, in any event, was often portrayed as little more than bandits, and if I wanted to fight there, I had better go soon or it would be over.

So I went. A lot of us did. More than one might think today. It was not a matter of any threat to this country. We all knew that. It was not a matter of any wartime-induced hatred of an enemy. It was something a male citizen of military age did, and nothing more.

The 9th Infantry Division that the army was building just then holds the record for the quickest activation and deployment to combat in American history. That record probably will never be broken. Fort Riley, Kansas, was empty since the 1st Infantry Division had already gone to Vietnam. The army made a skeleton unit with NCOs and officers drawn from all over the world, then filled up the ranks with trainees. We were C Company, 4th Battalion, 47th Infantry from the first day forward.

We trained hard that spring, summer and fall of 1966. The training was over in December. Nearly everybody got leave time to go home for Christmas. On 4 January 1967 the main body of our brigade left Fort Riley railhead bound for Oakland, California. A lot of soldiers' families had come to see them off. It must have been terribly hard for them to say goodbye there. Still, there was something reassuringly familiar in it: flatcars loaded with jeeps and deuce-and-a-halfs, and armored personnel carriers, and GIs with duffel bags getting aboard the troop cars – it was little different from what our fathers had done in the big war.

A couple of days later those of us in the "advance party" (company and battalion commanders, and a lot of platoon leader lieutenants and NCOs) got on board Air Force C-141 cargo jets, the big hump-shouldered four-engine jobs, to make the flight to Vietnam by way of Alaska and Japan. The main body would board troop ships and spend nearly two weeks at sea.

You cannot put your finger on *esprit-de-corps* but it is real. Without being aware of it, we had acquired it during the months of training together. There had not been a single AWOL after the Christmas leaves, and we believed that we were ready and our morale was very high. It was Kansas winter when we loaded the C-141s, and after about 24 hours of flight time, we got off into the heavy tropical air of Vietnam. It was like walking into a warm, damp blanket. It was a bit past midnight, and the first breaths of Vietnam were a mix of jet exhaust, jungle, and honest-to-god live artillery fire. We could see occasional tracers like red meteors on the horizon in any direction. We were in the War Zone.

For three weeks or so we ran short operations out of an established base camp called Bear Cat. This was dry forest country that might have been Missouri, except for the heat and the size of some of the trees. We did not know it at the time, but it was also in a province where there were almost no enemy units. The time we spent here was time allotted for getting used to the climate and for learning the basics of navigating the terrain.

One day in February we left for Dong Tam in the Mekong Delta. This was the 9th Division's new base camp near My Tho, built by dredging the Mekong mud and pumping it into rice paddies to make dry ground. When we got there, we carried our duffel bags to the edge of the piled-up mud, tossed them down, and that was the perimeter defense. Within a few months, Dong Tam would be more than 600 acres, and General Westmoreland called it the place where you could be up to your knees in mud, and have dust blow in your eyes.

Down in the Delta is where the dying began. We had lost some men up to this time, a few to booby traps, some to accidents, and a few more to gunshot wounds, but we were intact, really. We were the same battalion that had left Kansas. Now we met real enemy units, in company and battalion size, got into day-long fights, and lost people in serious numbers. By late spring more than two-thirds of our original men were gone, either killed or wounded badly enough for evacuation.

There is no training that prepares a soldier for all of this. The shocking violence and visual horrors of infantry fighting are far beyond anything imaginable. Now we learned the cost, not just the known cost of casualties, but the cost of having trained together and become buddies. When we lost men, we lost brothers. Week after week, until the weeks were months, we lost friends, much of the time in ways too ugly to describe. The losses get to you sooner or later.

Sooner or later you realize that the real objective is simply survival. I was a squad leader, and I keenly felt the responsibility for the lives of my men. The military mission did not matter much by this time. I would do what they told me to do, but no more, and that I would do as safely as possible. But it was impossible to keep everybody safe. I lost men anyway.

One of the terrible things about war is that it consumes the soul. When a close friend is killed or maybe has a leg blown off only feet away, it makes you sick with fear, and you rage inside at the waste and tragedy, and yet … and yet … from somewhere inside you hear a tiny voice saying, "Better him than me," and you know that it is true, and you know that you will do anything, anything at all to stay alive. War burns away the veneer of what we call civilization, and shows you that the last 10,000 years really had not made much difference in what we are.

Losing men to wounds is one thing. Killing is quite another. The killing is the worst part of war. The memory of it never goes away. There is little to say about this, because it is utterly removed from any other human experience, and there are no comparisons to make. It is the killing that haunts me the most.

More than three decades since I fought there, Vietnam is still close to the surface for me. I remember the men and the battles and the horror and the ugliness and the fear. I see much of it every night before I sleep, and still have nightmares about it. Much of my life stopped in 1967. Perhaps it might have been different. Maybe it did not have to turn out so miserably. All such thoughts are idle, of course. The only thing that matters, after all, is that we learned from our experience. I think we did.

You cannot put your finger on Post-traumatic Stress Disorder either, but it is real too. I had not heard the term until an army psychiatrist told me that I had it. Knowing there was a name for it did not do much good, but at least it was a start. The army discharged me because of PTSD, but when I turned to the Veterans Administration for some kind of help, I was told that the VA did not recognize it. It was a sad and frustrating time.

Today I understand myself a lot better. I would rather live than die, and that is an improvement. I have always been secretly proud of my service in Vietnam, and I am glad that I went. Americans learned a hell of a lot during the Vietnam years, and I had the privilege of being a part of it. I am not sorry.

John Young served as Squad Leader in the 9th Infantry in the Mobile Riverine Force in the

Mekong Delta in 1967. He holds the Combat Infantryman's Badge, three Bronze Stars for valor, a Purple Heart, two Air Medals and the Vietnamese Cross for Gallantry

John Young on his return to Vietnam with a mixed group of veterans and students in 2001. Here Young returns to a battlefield in the Mekong Delta and meets a Viet Cong adversary who he had fought against in 1967.
(John Young)

A nation divided

At the dawn of the 1960s Americans stood united and self-assured behind their charismatic young president, John F. Kennedy. Americans were certain that their leaders were good, honest men and that the nation as a whole was capable of no wrong. Confident in the future and in their own inherent decency most Americans looked to the new decade as a time of almost unlimited potential. However, below the surface of American politics tides of change were already churning, resulting in an unprecedented nexus of social transformation and upheaval that would threaten to rip the nation asunder. Powerful in their own right, the social movements of the 1960s became intertwined with the controversies surrounding the Vietnam War. Though it was quite possibly the most important event of the time period, the Vietnam War was inexorably linked to events on the American home front. Without understanding the 1960s, one cannot understand the American backlash against the war in Vietnam.

Album cover from Country Joe and the Fish. The music of the counterculture often took the lead in criticizing the war in Vietnam. (TRH Pictures)

Baby Boomers and the counterculture

During the 1960s the massive post-Second World War "baby boom" generation came of age. In their unprecedented millions baby boomers, possessed of a wealth and power that came to define their generation, became a catalyst for social change. Nearly every generation rebels against the control of their seniors but the baby boomers had the numbers and money that previous generations had lacked. Pampered by a nation that valued their spending power, the baby boomers were bent on testing the limits of societal control. In a postmodern flurry boomers questioned their parents' music, their economic morals, their beliefs, and their war.

The baby boomers that chose rebellion over conformity were referred to loosely as members of the "counterculture." Though an amorphous group the counterculture became intertwined with the growing antiwar movement as the decade of the 1960s progressed – a relationship that found expression in music. Led by groups such as the Beatles and the Rolling Stones, rock-and-roll spoke for the hopes and dreams of an entire generation. Illustrated most clearly by the concert at Woodstock in 1969 musicians sometimes even tried to lead social change, rather than serve as its reporters. Songs such as "Stand" by Sly and the Family Stone questioned race values. Several important songs, including "Purple Haze" by Jimi Hendrix, promoted the use of drugs. Other songs propounded the generational call to peace and harmony, epitomized in "Imagine" by John Lennon. Most disturbing to many, though, was the increasing number of songs that spoke directly against US involvement in the Vietnam War. Such music crossed barriers of color and style and included such important songs as "Fortunate Son" by Creedence Clearwater Revival and "What's Goin' On" by Marvin Gaye. In 1965 the older generation had been calmed to see the martial and patriotic "Ballad of the Green Berets" by Sergeant Barry Sadler spend weeks as the number one hit. By 1968, though, rock-and-roll had changed course, leading to songs like "I Feel Like I'm Fixin' to Die Rag" by Country Joe McDonald, which openly questioned the US involvement in Vietnam.

Members of the counterculture also experimented with "mind expanding" drugs, dabbled in free love, and toyed with the ideals of communism. To many young people the decade of the 1960s represented a time to question everything and believe in nothing. The resulting social cacophony led members of the counterculture in a bewildering number of different directions, injuring the political unity and importance of the proponents of change. Some young people chose to stand against American

policies, including the Vietnam War, and joined groups such as the Students for a Democratic Society and the Weathermen. Others chose to "turn on and drop out," becoming hippies who were too busy rejecting society to bother with rejecting society's war. Still other groups occupied a middle ground (including the Yippies) who gleefully backed the candidacy of a pig for president in 1968. Most young people, though, affiliated with no particular group in the 1960s and occupied the distant fringes of the counterculture. These baby boomers enjoyed the music of the time and were even part-time protesters but also remained in college and part of the American dream.

Perhaps the most controversial element of the Vietnam War to the baby boom generation was the draft system. The looming threat of service in Vietnam seemed constant, but was imminently avoidable through its numerous available loopholes, or deferments. Most importantly college students were deferred from the draft. Universities across the United States

Draft resisters rally in San Francisco. The inequities of the draft system during the Vietnam War helped unify antiwar factions in a disparate society. (TRH Pictures)

exploded in size as young people rushed to take advantage of this legal way to avoid service in Vietnam. For those who chose not to go to college other forms of deferment existed. Joining the National Guard, getting a letter from a sympathetic doctor or working in one of the many exempt industries all kept young men out of the controversial war. Thus men in the United States with connections or money could avoid being drafted. Protected by their deferments and from the relative safety of college campuses many baby boomers demonstrated their dislike for the Vietnam War through marches and protests. During the Vietnam era antiwar protests became commonplace and often erupted into violence. The ongoing protest did much to polarize the country, but the true verdict of the baby boom generation on the Vietnam War, though, was more subtle and can be illustrated through simple numbers. During the conflict some three million young men and women served in Vietnam while over 15 million chose to avoid service, mainly through legal draft deferments.

Civil rights and the Great Society

The most powerful force for social change in the United States during the 1960s was the emerging Civil Rights Movement. Since the failure of Reconstruction black citizens of the United States, especially in the deep south, had lived under a system of segregation known as "Jim Crow." Nearly a century later forces of racial toleration and equality marshaled their strength, aided by the 1954 landmark Supreme Court decision in *Brown vs Board of Education* that declared segregation in public schools to be unconstitutional, so bringing the entire system of segregation into question. Across the south whites rallied their forces to defend their social system, while African-Americans began to test their newfound rights.

In Birmingham, Alabama, Reverend Martin Luther King, Jr. emerged as the leader of the Civil Rights Movement amid a black boycott of the city's segregated bus system. King chose to rely upon nonviolent protest to achieve his goals, following the example of Ghandi. Across the south African-Americans began to practice peaceful civil disobedience, including protests and sit-ins, methods that would later be co-opted by the antiwar movement. Whites retaliated, often violently; civil rights leaders were assassinated and marchers were beaten, sometimes by the police who were supposed to defend them. During the ongoing process King and other civil rights leaders made masterful use of television coverage and Americans watched the nightly news in horror as police dogs attacked peaceful protesters.

While African-Americans attempted to help themselves, government actions exacerbated the tense situation. Belated attempts at school desegregation led to violent clashes, most notably in Little Rock, Arkansas, and at the University of Mississippi. In both cases National Guard units had to be called out to hold local whites at bay while black students attended classes. The resulting struggle at the University of Mississippi raged for an entire day and caused several deaths. It seemed that America was being torn apart along racial lines. After the massive "March on Washington," during which King encapsulated the goals of the Civil Right's Movement in his famous "I have a dream" speech, the US government responded. President Johnson guided through congress the Civil Rights Act, which outlawed segregation, and the Voting Rights Act which enfranchised America's African-American citizens.

The Civil Rights struggle was not yet over, for African-Americans still met widespread violence and prejudice. In addition, following centuries of hardship many African-Americans remained poor, often confined to decaying inner city environments. King and others now attempted to seek economic change. Most Americans were reluctant to part with their hard-earned money and change came only

The societal upheavals in America during the 1960s nearly ripped the nation apart – damaging the American consensus for war. Here Reverend Martin Luther King Jr. is shown on the steps of the Lincoln Memorial during the march on Washington. (Topham Picturepoint)

slowly. President Johnson supported expansion of the American Dream to include African-Americans and made economic and social change, what he called the "Great Society," the centerpiece of his presidency. The pace of change, though, was slow and infuriated black leaders. As a result King found himself losing control of elements of the Civil Rights Movement, and many African-Americans opted instead for militancy, joining more radical groups such as the Black Panthers.

The mounting price tag of the war in Vietnam slowed the pace of economic change in the United States, frustrating several African-American leaders, including King. In 1967 King began to speak out against the Vietnam War as a waste of American lives and a misuse of American money that could be set aside to help the needy. Other African-American leaders saw the Vietnam War in even more stark racial terms. Led by Elijah Muhammed the Nation of Islam spoke out against the war. Why were oppressed American citizens of color fighting in Vietnam to oppress other citizens of color? Why were a disproportionate number of the fighting men in Vietnam black? To many African-Americans the conflict in Vietnam seemed to be the white man's war but the black man's fight. One popular quote from the 1960s was, "No Viet Cong ever called me Nigger." Thus by 1967 the Civil Rights Movement and the Vietnam War had crossed paths – illustrated by the case of Muhammed Ali. When drafted the talented heavyweight champion chose to seek conscientious objector status on religious grounds as a member of the Nation of Islam. His case was rejected, but he still refused to serve, choosing instead to speak out against the war in racial terms. Stripped of his heavyweight crown, Ali sacrificed five years of his career to a series of legal battles, becoming a de facto leader of the antiwar movement in the process.

In April 1968 an assassin's bullet destroyed the fragile unity and flagging hopes of civil rights leaders. Martin Luther King's death in Memphis threw the nation into disarray and resulted in violent riots in over 130 major American cities, an ironic consequence of the death of such a gentle

man. Racial violence across the nation merged with growing antiwar protest and violence in the wake of the Tet Offensive. To many observers the nearly constant rioting and protests seemed to presage a second American Revolution. Johnson, recently convinced that his war in Vietnam had been lost, now saw his Great Society in tatters as well. The combination was simply too much and forced Johnson out of politics. As a result the conservative Richard Nixon won the presidential election of 1968. Though he continued the Vietnam War, Nixon put an end to the Civil Rights Movement. The new president and his massive constituency longed for an end of the constant upheavals of the 1960s and to put a stop to the continuation of social change. In addition

Nixon succeeded in reducing antiwar feeling by shifting the draft to a more equitable lottery system. Possibly most important, though, was the onset of a recession in the United States. Distracted by their economic woes, and yearning for a return to normality most Americans began to ignore the dwindling war in Vietnam and the social wars of the 1960s ground to a halt.

Social change and the Vietnam War had interacted in many ways. The war had caused social unrest and helped to undermine the success of the Civil Rights Movement. In turn political turmoil on the home front had done much to limit American use of force in Vietnam, possibly even making the war there unwinnable. Thus the two powerful forces of the 1960s both fed off of each other and in the end destroyed each other. The United States would lose the Vietnam War long after most protesters had ceased to care. Along with Vietnam the hopes and dreams of the counterculture and the Civil Rights Movement lay in ruins. The world had not been changed and African-Americans would have to engage in a continuing struggle to obtain an equal place in American society. As President Johnson surveyed the wreckage of his policy in 1968 he judged the situation well and in harsh terms by saying, "That bitch Vietnam has killed the woman I loved, the Great Society."

An army rejected

The United States military force that had entered Vietnam in 1965 was the finest in the world. The prolonged war, augmented by social upheaval, had altered the situation dramatically by the close of the decade. Most of the professional soldiers had long since left Vietnam to be replaced by draftees. Though most draftees still fought hard and well, they could not fail to represent the country that they had been taken from, one that was turning against the Vietnam War. Many draftees were politically aware African-Americans, who were often forced to mix with whites from the rural south. The situation was often tense, especially so in rear areas and sometimes even resulted in racially motivated firefights.

US soldiers in Vietnam by 1970 were painfully aware that their nation had abandoned them and that the United States was withdrawing from the conflict. They were being asked to fight a war that most people avoided, many people hated and that the country had no intention of winning. The morale of the US military in Vietnam plummeted. Small unit cohesion, already damaged by the one-year tour of duty policy, suffered greatly. Many soldiers rejected sacrificing their lives for a lost war and came into Vietnam with only one idea, surviving for a single year and returning home. Entire units began to sabotage orders and practice "search and evade" tactics designed to minimize contact with the enemy. Some soldiers saw their own officers and non-commissioned officers as a threat to their survival. Officers who intended to make a career out of the army, known as "lifers," sometimes forced reluctant soldiers to do their duty. Making matters worse was the practice of rotating officers out of a combat slot after only six months. As a result many officers in Vietnam were inexperienced and, thus, dangerous. Due to this potent mixture US forces in Vietnam began to suffer from increased incidents of "fragging," in which soldiers attempted to assassinate their own officers or non-commissioned officers. In 1969 the army reported 96 cases of fragging, and the number shot up to an astounding 209 cases in 1970.

Another indictor of flagging morale was increased drug use. Drugs were cheap and readily available throughout South Vietnam, supplied sometimes as a service by the communists in an effort to incapacitate American soldiers. By 1970 this had led to a problem of epidemic proportions. A battalion exit poll indicated that 60 percent of enlisted men had used marijuana during their tour of duty, with 35 percent of those polled admitting to using the drug more than 200 times. It was heroin, though, that

Lieutenant William Calley. (TRH Pictures)

posed the most serious problem. Viet Cong operatives sometimes supplied marijuana cigarettes to American solders free of charge but laced the cigarettes with heroin, hoping to enmesh the soldier in a cycle of addiction. By 1971 the heroin problem had spiraled out of control and the army admitted that some 35,000 soldiers in Vietnam were addicts.

The best known indicator that the Vietnam War had taken a toll on the effectiveness of the US military was the My Lai Massacre. On 16 March 1968 men of "C" Company, 1st Battalion, 11th Infantry Brigade murdered over 300 unarmed civilians in the village of My Lai in Quang Ngai Province. In a highly publicized trial, Lieutenant William Calley, a platoon leader of "C" Company, was eventually convicted of mass murder and sent to prison. Though he served but three years of his sentence, many saw Calley as a scapegoat for a war gone wrong. Calley, though, was not representative of the United States Army. The vast majority of soldiers in Vietnam were draftees who served their country with valor under the most trying of circumstances. They fought on and sacrificed and died for a nation that no longer believed in their cause. That the problems with atrocities, drug use and fraggings existed at all, though, indicates that the military in Vietnam was in serious trouble. At the close of the war the morale of the US military was at its lowest point ever, and it would not be until the Gulf War that the military would restore its battered reputation.

The effects of the war on Vietnam

While the United States seemed to teeter on the brink of a new revolution, the war had a much more direct and devastating effect on the people and country of Vietnam. Though the Vietnam War was, in many ways, a colonial war that had been transformed into a superpower conflict, it also was a vicious civil war, pitting the Vietnamese against each other. Thus the Vietnam War was an ideological struggle for the Vietnamese, one that would not end with an American departure from the conflict. As with most civil wars, the fighting in Vietnam would linger for years and involve a thorough retribution on the part of the victors.

The effects of the conflict were more immediate to many within Vietnam as war visited the countryside spreading unprecedented levels of death and destruction. While NVA and VC forces were brutal, often using terror and assassination as weapons, their effect on the country and its people – though insidious – was militarily limited until late in the conflict. US and ARVN forces, though, fought a technological war, using lavish fire power support as a force multiplier. Though in some areas US forces severely curtailed their use of firepower in an effort to minimize civilian casualties, both North and South Vietnam suffered from the heaviest bombing in the history of warfare. In 1967 alone in Binh Dinh Province of South Vietnam attack helicopters fired 131,000 shells, warships fired 5,100 shells, while bombers carpeted the area with 8.5 million pounds of explosives and 500,000 pounds of napalm. American air power, the trump card of the war, ranged across the countries of Southeast Asia. During the conflict US air power dropped 450,000 tons of bombs on Laos, 430,000 tons of bombs on Cambodia, 643,000 tons of bombs on North Vietnam (not including Operations Linebacker I and II) and 700,000 tons of bombs on South Vietnam – far exceeding the total bomb tonnage dropped by all sides in the Second World War.

One especially controversial element of the US war in Vietnam was Operation Ranch Hand – the defoliation program. Part of the US effort at counterinsurgency Ranch Hand represented an attempt to deny cover and sustenance to the Viet Cong. American forces used a variety of chemical herbicides, identified by their colored containers, to achieve their goals. Fast-acting Agent Blue was the preferred herbicide for crops, while Agent Orange was preferred for forested areas. Though there were many dispersal systems for the defoliants the most effective were converted C-123 aircraft. Fitted with special nozzles a single C-123 could spread defoliant on a 300-acre area in only four minutes. The pilots of Operation Ranch Hand, whose motto was "Only you can prevent forests," performed their task well, eventually dumping over 19 million gallons of chemical poisons over six million acres of land in South Vietnam and affecting more than 20 percent of the entire country.

In real terms Operation Ranch Hand had scant effect on enemy forces, who always found new sanctuaries and sources of supply. Controversy dogged the program, for many believed that the dioxin-based herbicides presented tremendous health risks. After receiving proof of the danger of dioxin use, the Defense Department in 1970 ordered a halt to Operation Ranch Hand but the damage had been done. US veterans of the conflict complaining of serious health problems eventually settled their grievances with a reluctant government out of court in 1985. In South Vietnam the damage was indescribable, leaving many civilians to live in a toxic environment and leading to untold thousands of birth defects and deaths.

The Montagnards

Montagnards, or hill people, are indigenous people of the Central Highlands of Vietnam. Tribal in nature the Montagnards practice subsistence agriculture and view themselves as separate from the Vietnamese, who often refer to the Montagnards as "moi" or savages. During the Vietnam War Montagnard forces were recruited for both sides and formed the backbone of the Civilian Irregular Defense Group allied with the US Special Forces. Montagnard troops proved to be fierce fighters and quickly earned the respect of their American advisors and counterparts,

A Montagnard woman and her children in their home in 2001. Even to this day the Montagnards continue to resist a Vietnamese cultural takeover. (Author's collection)

often taking part in the most dangerous missions into Cambodia and Laos. The Montagnard participation in the Vietnam War, though, proved catastrophic for them. Of a total population of only one million almost 200,000 Montagnards died in the conflict. Their lands, located in the critical border area, were often designated "free fire zones" leading to a resettlement of nearly 85 percent of the entire population. At the close of the conflict the communists exacted retribution against their Montagnard enemies, removing many of the remaining Montagnards from their ancestral lands to make way for Vietnamese settlers. Some Montagnard fighters continued to resist Vietnamese domination, with one armed unit only choosing to flee in 1993. Today relations between the Vietnamese and the Montagnards remain tense in some areas, still erupting into violence stemming from the Vietnam War.

Laos

Before the fall of Dien Bien Phu Americans had identified Laos as a test for their

Ruins in Hanoi in the wake of Operation Linebacker II.
(TRH Pictures/ US Air Force)

containment strategy. The royalist Lao
government in Vientiane faced a major
threat from a Soviet-backed communist
insurgent force known as the Pathet Lao. At
first US support for the Laotian government
took the form of military aid and advisors,
but as war loomed in Vietnam the situation

changed dramatically, for the North Vietnamese intervened in Laotian affairs, partly to secure the Ho Chi Minh Trail. The resulting infusion of forces served to tip the delicate balance toward the Pathet Lao in the ongoing civil war in Laos. As a result the United States began to play a more direct role in the struggle. Unlike the war in South Vietnam, the American war in Laos was a "secret" one – largely fought and directed under the auspices of the Central Intelligence Agency.

CIA operatives, who despaired of the ability of the Royal Lao Army, searched for other allies in the struggle against communism in Laos and discovered the Hmong. One of several Montagnard tribes, the Hmong inhabit northern Laos along the border with Vietnam. Fiercely independent the Hmong saw both the Pathet Lao and the North Vietnamese as threats and readily agreed to join with US and Laotian government forces against the communists. By 1961 the CIA had raised and armed a force of over 10,000 Hmong tribesmen in an effort to even the odds. As the war progressed the Hmong irregular forces, under the command of General Vang Pao, became the most effective fighting force allied to the United States, facing down communist attacks on the strategic Plain of Jars. The daring Hmong tribesmen, supplied by the CIA, operated Air America and augmented by Thai troops, also performed several other duties including surveillance of the Ho Chi Minh Trail and secret forays into North Vietnam itself. Aided by devastating American air strikes the Hmong and Royal Lao forces fought the communists to a standstill and the war in Laos proceeded as a bloody stalemate.

By 1970, though, the momentum had shifted in the "Secret War" in Laos. The Hmong, worn down by years of bloody fighting, had lost 10,000 dead while 100,000 were forced to flee their shattered villages as refugees. Though it had fought bravely, and had even resorted to drafting children, Vang Pao's Hmong army had been defeated in a war of attrition. Though a peace treaty was signed in 1971 the North Vietnamese and the Pathet Lao kept the pressure on their hated Hmong enemies and engaged in brutal ethnic cleansing. Abandoned by their powerful allies some Hmong fought on, while others fled the country in an attempt to reach the United States. Only after the final fall of Laos in 1975 did life for the Hmong return to a semblance of normality. The Hmong culture, and much of Laotian society as a whole, had nearly ceased to exist – having been caught between the warring sides in the Vietnam War.

Cambodia

The seizure of power by General Lon Nol and the subsequent allied invasion had thrown the nation of Cambodia into turmoil. Long moribund the insurgency of the Khmer Rouge gained in popularity – even claiming the adherence of Prince Sihanouk. In addition NVA forces in the country, eager to protect the vital Ho Chi Minh Trail, placed further military pressure on the Lon Nol regime. Though US monetary aid to the Cambodian government increased as a result it was, in general, a time of American disengagement from the war, leaving Lon Nol's forces alone to face the combined might of the Khmer Rouge and the NVA.

By 1973 Cambodian government forces were reeling in the face of the onslaught and fell back to a defense of the capital city of Phnom Penh, abandoning 70 percent of the countryside to the hands of the Khmer Rouge. Loathe to witness the fall of Cambodia, though, US forces unleashed B-52 strikes on the Khmer Rouge attackers with devastating results. Phnom Penh had been saved but at a tremendous cost. The heavy bombing and nearly continuous fighting had shattered the already weak Cambodian economy and had killed more than 100,000 people. Lon Nol had little to defend but weary bands of refugees.

Battered and enraged the Khmer Rouge forces, led by the mercurial Saloth Sar (alias

Pol Pot – leader of the Khmer Rouge and architect of the ruthless societal holocaust in Cambodia known as the "Killing Fields." (Topham Picturepoint)

Pol Pot), awaited their next opportunity to seize power. Upon the signing of the Paris Peace Accords in 1973 a rift developed between the Khmer Rouge and their North Vietnamese allies. Pol Pot and others felt betrayed that the NVA had left the fight and harbored an animosity that would erupt into war in January 1979. Partly as a result of the events of 1973 the Khmer Rouge purged its more moderate elements and became the most radical communist force in Southeast Asia, adhering to an agrarian form of Marxism and hoping to destroy urban and intellectual life in favor of "simple" peasant life. In 1975 the reformulated Khmer Rouge stood ready once again to assault Phnom Penh. By this time the United States had lost interest in the war – meaning that the B-52s would not return. On 17 April, realizing that his country was doomed, Lon Nol surrendered and the Khmer Rouge made ready to begin their terrible reformation of Cambodian society.

Kim Herzinger

Everybody has something to say about the 1960s, and it should be made clear now that my say does not have the legitimacy of someone who was centrally involved in the antiwar movement, the civil rights movement, the counterculture, or any of the other movements and compulsions which have since come to define the period. I never led a march, I never spoke at a protest, I never attempted to levitate the Pentagon. I went to some vigils and stood silently, I went to a few sit-ins and sat-in. I was hosed just twice, and one of those times for reasons understandable even to me. I was not a freedom rider, I never walked with Martin Luther King, or went to Washington. I did not live in Haight-Ashbury, never went to India to see the Maharishi, and I was absent at Woodstock. I was a *part* of the 1960s, yes, but I was not one of those who *made* the 1960s. Still, the testimony of the mere participant is still testimony, and all the more significant because there are so many of us who followed, so few of us who led.

First, it should be said that no specific feature of the 1960s can be definitively separated from any other feature. The ideas and emotions that motivated the antiwar movement cannot be successfully separated from those associated with the civil rights movement; and the bumptious rebellion of the counterculture cannot be successfully separated from either. What connected all of these movements and tendencies was that each emerged out of a century-long argument with established assumptions, beliefs, and traditions, and that each, in wildly different ways and using wildly different methods, desired to fulfill the promise, to make real the possibilities, that seemed to be newly available to our generation.

The late 1960s was dream time for the visionary sensibility, and although its arguments during that time were primarily emotional, and only occasionally practical, ethical, or theological, it is perhaps the only sensibility that could make sense of the widely shared feeling among many that the time had finally come when everything was possible, and that we were living in a charmed moment of universal liberation, a time of unbinding energies.

Kim Herzinger as a college student in 1969 just after his decision to become a conscientious objector to the Vietnam War. (Kim Herzinger)

By 1966, I was firmly and insistently opposed to the war in Vietnam. By then, a number of things seemed true. First, that the Vietnamese were engaged in a civil war, and the side we were backing—non-communist, perhaps, but oily and blatantly corrupt—was being opposed for very good reasons indeed. Second, our government had begun to lie to us about the war on a consistent basis—about its reasons for our being there, about when the war might end, about our acceptance among the Vietnamese people, about what we were doing and why we were doing it. Third, our suspicions about deep-seated American racism, which had been brought into such sharp focus at home, seemed to be being replicated in Vietnam. The language and treatment of the Vietnamese—friend or foe, when we could tell the difference—only confirmed what we thought was worst in the structure of American ideas and attitudes. Fourth, television was making it quite clear that what we were doing in Vietnam was invalid, badly executed, wasteful, vicious, and ugly. It was no longer possible to watch the nightly news without having to confront the fact that Americans were apparently capable of the kinds of atrocities we had not thought imaginable. What we knew about war had come mainly from World War II movies. We had looked very good in them, and the evil we were confronting then was clear to all. We did not look so good burning down villages, spreading napalm over the countryside, setting—indiscriminately, it seemed—women and children on fire in order to secure a rice paddy or a clutch of straw huts. The incident at My Lai seemed only the most dramatic example of the fruit of a wrong-headed, racist, and vicious American policy. Finally, there was the draft, surely the most ill-begotten and dysfunctional system ever devised for use in an unpopular war. The draft was the sword upstairs, and it hung over everyone's head, descending, about to descend, always ready to descend, on every young male neck in America.

It was with the draft that the Establishment, under suspicion as illegitimate when it came to exercising its wrath and self-interest in our name, was insisting on its power to coerce precisely those people who were most inclined to resist every kind of coercive power – a generation particularly given to confrontation, one that felt marginalized by traditional authority and chafed by traditional cultural habits and attitudes, dominated by political, social, and cultural confrontations with authority, and participants in an active counterculture which celebrated its rebelliousness, its outsider status, its marginality.

By 1966, America was becoming a nation divided into Us and Them. And the Vietnam War's capacity to harden everything had become clear to everyone. It was not a time that inspired sympathies for those who did not share one's beliefs and attitudes, just as it did not inspire reasoned discourse. The era inflamed everything; everything was fraught with significance. To take a stand was the most important stand to take. Sides were chosen with the kind of religious fervor that can tolerate only the smallest disagreements. Tolerance was recognized as admirable, but often only when one was arguing that it was his particular position that should be tolerated, not the other way around.

It was easy to be smug and righteous about being a dissenter. Too easy. I was smug because I was sure I was right, righteous because what I was right about was a cause that required the conversion of others and the active participation of those converts in the cause. I do not mean to suggest by this that I now think I was wrong about the war. Indeed, I do not think I was wrong, and the historical evidence only further convinces me that I was not wrong. But I was very likely right for a lot of wrong reasons and, in any case, the smugness and righteousness that I and most of my fellow dissenters put chronically on show now makes me queasy. At the time, though, it was perhaps inevitable, perhaps even indispensable. I could carry a sign with the best of them.

And then, sometime in 1967, I decided to do something that was, actually, quite outside the norm—hardly singular, but still relatively rare. I applied to become a conscientious objector.

I am somewhat mystified to this day as to why I applied for conscientious objector status. Perhaps I wanted to know exactly what my situation would be after I graduated and was eminently draftable. Perhaps I wanted to make a separate peace with myself, my family, and my conscience. Certainly I believed conscientiously in the arguments for nonviolence, and though the question of whether or not I would have proclaimed pacifism in the face of Hitler and Hirohito was indeed a worrisome one, it seemed to me that it was *because* of World War II, *because* of the bomb, that pacifism was now a reasonable, perhaps even necessary, position. Whatever the case, along with the idea of implicitly agreeing to the dictates of a government I distrusted, the most horrifying idea was that I might be ordered to join the army, go to Vietnam, and kill people.

But to apply for a C. O. presented its own problems. I was absolutely under the impression that to apply and fail practically guaranteed my being drafted at the earliest possible moment. It was at the very least generally recognized that putting your name in front of the draft board for any reason at all was an incredibly stupid thing to do. It was understood that government agents scanned photographs of antiwar protests and then sent pictures of the participants to draft boards with recommendations for immediate call-up. And though many stories that circulated among the already deferred can be attributed to the endemic paranoia of the time, paranoids too can have real enemies. My subscription copy of *Ramparts* magazine, I began to notice sometime in 1968, had been regularly steamed open somewhere along its mail route.

I don't remember thinking then, nor do I think now, that I was taking a particularly noble stand. I certainly thought it nobler than pretending to be gay or crazy or drugged-out, and without doubt nobler than joining the National Guard—and all of these were much ballyhooed methods of eluding induction – but I can't say I thought it nobler than going to Canada or burning my draft card on General Hershey's front lawn. I certainly did not apply to achieve a deferment, at least an immediate one. The fact of the matter was that everybody in college was already deferred from the draft as a matter of course, and I had two years of college to go. I am quite amazed at the number of people, people who know better, who are willing to maintain publicly that accepting a college deferment was draft-dodging. Throughout the Vietnam War, everyone knew what a draft-dodger was, and it wasn't some guy going to college. Whoever they were, and no matter how academically deficient, unless they flunked out or dropped out, college students were deferred; everybody knew it and everybody accepted it.

Applying for a C. O., then, was an act that might have consequences beyond the required 24 consecutive months of government-approved work that would begin after graduation. But what was understood to be acceptable pacifism by the government usually involved the evidence of an historical pattern of pacifism, based firmly in what the government considered to be acceptable religious traditions. My family had no history of pacifism, the church I was then affiliated with was not historically pacifist, and the truth of the matter was that I should not have had a chance in Hue to be accepted as a C. O. by my hometown draft board. The form I was required to fill out hardly inspired confidence. Every question was directed in such a way as to discover the nature of the applicant's belief in a Supreme Being, his specifically religious objections to war, and to establish whether or not the applicant's pacifism applied to all forms of violence, or was simply limited to specific wars that he objected to for no better reasons than whim or fright. My answers, though they certainly referred to and quoted everything from the *New Testament* to the *Bhagavad Gita*, relied rather too heavily, I thought, on Gandhi, Thoreau, Martin Luther King, and relevant quotes from *Bartlett's*.

I applied in late 1967, and sometime in 1968 I received a letter from my draft board and read, with some surprise but more relief, that I was now officially no longer a college deferment; I was now officially a Conscientious Objector. Gandhi, Thoreau, King, and *Bartlett's* had wielded more power than I imagined possible.

Now, when I am hauled up before a class as a relic of the 1960s, willing if not necessarily able to describe the shifting sensations and edgy paranoia of that time, what I am least capable of explaining is why it was that the sides were so inflexible, why it was that those who supported the war, indeed those who fought in it, were understood to be the enemy. I experienced no communion with the soldiers who were packed off to Vietnam, and none with the soldiers who managed to return. Worse, other than the strong sense that those who went off to fight had been hoodwinked by an evil system and an evil policy, I experienced no sympathy for them either. To have felt enmity toward all the old men who were running the show and, perhaps

especially, those who became their representatives—police, politicians, and almost anyone who represented the "Establishment"—is, I think, at least understandable. But such disdain for the soldiers—young men of my own age, after all, many of whom I would have ordinarily befriended—is far harder to understand.

These soldiers returned to a country full of people who loathed them because they had gone, distrusted them because they had lost, or simply wanted to forget them. They had lugged home what was left of themselves to accusations and indifference. It is shameful, of course, that returning soldiers were treated with such disdain, that the problems they returned with—personal, social, economic, psychological—were disregarded by the people they had thought they'd been fighting for, and by the government who sent them off to do it. At the time, however, at least for those of us who opposed the war, the soldier

Kim Herzinger in 2002 – as a Professor of English at the University of Southern Mississippi, Herzinger often works in tandem with John Young. (Kim Herzinger)

was the most dramatic representative of what we most despised; they were part of the problem, not the solution. Then, as now, but in an entirely different way, we could not separate the soldier from the war, their harrowing experience from our government's grotesque adventure. Now it seems evident that many people—especially those too young to have lived through the era – are entirely unable to distinguish their ideas and emotions about the Vietnam War from their ideas and emotions about the men who fought in it. This is inevitable, perhaps, but dangerous, too.

These sympathies are well placed and understandable, but they should not obscure the fact that the Vietnam War was a damn shame all the way around—a war and a place and a time where none of the available options were any good at all. It was the war that was the most shameful thing of all – badly conceived, badly executed, invalid, unjust, and unnecessary. Understanding for the soldiers who fought in it—too late, no doubt, and too little—cannot and should not obliterate our understanding of what that war was, how it scarred all of us, and how we should never allow ourselves another episode anything at all like it.

Kim Herzinger is a Professor of English at the University of Southern Mississippi and is the author of books on D. H. Lawrence and Donald Barthelme.

US withdrawal

The war in Vietnam did not end with American withdrawal from the conflict, it only changed. In 1973 the situation looked hopeful for the South Vietnamese. The ARVN was over one million strong and was the recipient of the very latest US weaponry, much of it simply left behind by their departing allies. The communists, though, still smarting from their recent defeats, had only 150,000 troops in South Vietnam. In addition the communist supply lines lay in ruins. The ARVN was in a dominant position but it was not to last long.

The South Vietnamese regime was weak and corrupt. President Thieu, in some ways the most effective president in South Vietnamese history, did little to win the all-important support of his own people. Thus the morale of the ARVN and the South Vietnamese people would remain in question as the crisis neared. Thieu believed, as did the North Vietnamese, that US forces would never abandon South Vietnam after having invested so much blood and wealth in its defense. In Washington, though, Congress passed the War Powers Act that called for congressional approval of any overseas troop deployment – effectively ending any hope that Nixon might have had regarding future military aid to Vietnam. Matters worsened in August 1974 when Nixon resigned rather than face impeachment over the Watergate scandal, to be replaced in office by President Gerald Ford. With no true mandate to govern Ford would not call for US troops to re-enter Vietnam. The South Vietnamese regime was on its own.

Aware that his advantage might be short lived Thieu immediately ordered the ARVN to take the offensive, and made nearly continuous gains. Beneath the surface veneer of success, though, the Saigon regime had already begun to collapse. Reliant upon mobility and firepower, the ARVN was an expensive, modern army that required an operation budget of nearly three billion dollars per year. The moribund South Vietnamese economy could come nowhere near paying for the ARVN, leaving South Vietnam almost totally reliant on US economic aid for its own defense. Making matters worse much of the aid money was siphoned off by an extremely corrupt regime. Amid lingering recession the American people became increasingly concerned with their own problems and began to cut monetary aid to South Vietnam. In 1973 the United States sent 2.3 billion dollars in aid to South Vietnam and cut aid to only 1.1 billion dollars in 1974. The drop in aid caused the South Vietnamese economy to implode. Inflation shot up over 200 percent, destroying the fledgling South Vietnamese middle class and causing widespread poverty and unrest. The South Vietnamese people had little reason to defend their nation.

President Thieu spoke out against the cutbacks, but did little to end the corruption of his government. As a result American aid, though significant, no longer even covered the costs of the ARVN, leading to a shortage of fuel, ammunition, and spare parts for their ultra-modern array of weaponry. By the end of the year the ARVN had lost its firepower edge over the NVA and even much of its mobility. Trucks, tanks, jets and helicopters lay disused at bases all over South Vietnam due to lack of fuel. The collapse of the South Vietnamese economy and military demonstrated that Nixon's policy of Vietnamization had been bankrupt. South Vietnam had not been made into a viable nation but the US had succeeded in exiting the war. Though it still remained strong on paper the ARVN was now immobile and nearly defenseless. The end was near.

North Vietnam attacks

By late 1974 the North Vietnamese had recovered from their losses in 1972 and stood ready to attack. Armed with the latest Soviet weaponry the NVA had worked hard to overcome its command and control problems and was eager to put an end to the conflict in Vietnam. Some members of the Politburo, though, believed an attack to be too risky. The ARVN appeared to be a formidable foe, and any major attack might cause renewed bombing by the United States. The impasse was broken by Le Duan, a Politburo member, who suggested a limited offensive against South Vietnam aimed at the seizure of Phuoc Long Province. Such an attack would serve to test the strength of the ARVN and would also test American resolve to return to the conflict.

In mid-December two NVA divisions, under the operational command of General Tran Van Tra moved forward to the attack. Short on ammunition and fuel the ARVN's resolve soon crumbled, and in only three weeks Phuoc Long Province had fallen. Of greatest importance was the fact that, though Thieu had called for support against communist aggression, the American B-52s had not returned to the fray and bombed the attack into dust. America would not return to Southeast Asia to defend its stricken ally. The mood in Hanoi was jubilant – one communist leader remarked that American forces would not return to the conflict in Vietnam, "even if we offered them candy." It was now deemed safe to launch the massive offensive designed finally to end the war.

The first phase of the general offensive began on 1 March under the operational command of General Van Tien Dung. Five NVA divisions attacked into the Central Highlands – supported by armor, artillery, and combat engineers. The ARVN in the area hoped to mount a staunch defense of Pleiku but quickly found themselves flanked by an NVA advance on the critical road junction town of Ban Me Thuot. Though ARVN defenders in the area resisted bravely they were heavily outnumbered and surrounded and within a week the town fell into enemy hands.

In the face of impending defeat President Thieu made one of his most important, and worst, decisions of the war. He ordered his forces in the Central Highlands to retreat to the coastal city of Tuy Hoa. Such a move required the ARVN to engage in a fighting withdrawal – one of the most difficult operations in warfare. Thieu hoped that his forces could regroup south of Tuy Hoa to defend Saigon, thereby sacrificing the northern half of South Vietnam to buy time. The move proved disastrous. Civilians and soldiers alike began to flee down the one main road of the Central Highlands and the retreat turned into a rout. Crammed with over 200,000 people the single road soon became hopelessly jammed. Artillery shells rained down on the fleeing mob, causing chaos and destruction as the rout became a disaster. During the horrific retreat nearly 100,000 people died or were captured by the NVA. Thieu's planning and his entire nation began to fall apart.

World Airways flight from Danang

The last flight to leave Danang was a World Airways 727, sent to rescue women and children from the coming holocaust. However, over 300 armed ARVN soldiers rushed the aircraft, trampling many of the women and children in the process. The frightened pilot moved to make a quick take off but found the aircraft under attack by ARVN soldiers who had been unable to board. Under fire and damaged by a grenade burst the aircraft lumbered into the sky. Once in the air the pilot realized that he could not retract the landing gear because several ARVN soldiers had taken refuge in the wheel wells of the aircraft. During the 90-minute flight to Saigon several of these desperate men plunged to their deaths but an unknown number gained their freedom. In Saigon the ARVN soldiers who exited the aircraft were greeted with cheers. It was later discovered that only five women and children ever made it on board the flight.

As disaster loomed in the Central Highlands five additional NVA divisions surged forward to attack the northern provinces of South Vietnam. Though some ARVN units resisted gallantly the situation quickly deteriorated, especially after units in the north realized that they had been cut off due to the retreat in the Central Highlands. All across the area soldiers and civilians alike streamed toward the coastal city of Danang with the hope that they could escape the coming cataclysm by sea. Nearly two million frantic refugees, including thousands of soldiers who had removed their uniforms to blend in with the civilian masses, deluged the city. Belatedly South Vietnamese authorities attempted a sea rescue but were only able to save 50,000 people before Danang fell under NVA control.

ABOVE President Thieu of South Vietnam, a corrupt and ineffective leader who wrongly believed that the US would not stand by and watch his regime crumble after so many years of sacrifice. (TRH Pictures)

RIGHT Sensing victory but fearing the return of the Americans the North Vietnamese initially attacked only Phuoc Long Province in December 1974. The province quickly fell – demonstrating ARVN weakness – and the American bombers did not return. As a result the North Vietnamese, who had learned much from their failed Easter Offensive, in March attacked the Central Highlands. Outflanked and outfought the ARVN defenders in the area – on the orders of President Thieu – fled for the coast and South Vietnam began to collapse. A second offensive struck near the DMZ also met with great success – causing a mass exodus of refugees from the area. Barely a month after the attacks began the ARVN fought a gallant but doomed defense of Xuan Loc – at the very gates of Saigon. Days later, though, on 30 April Saigon fell and the war in Vietnam finally came to an end.

The Ho Chi Minh campaign

Across South Vietnam NVA forces converged on Saigon and victory. The North Vietnamese, eager to press their advantage and seize Saigon before the onset of the monsoon season, quickly launched the Ho Chi Minh

Campaign. In early April the ARVN 18th Division, under the command of General Le Ming Dao, stood firm in the defense of the critical road junction of Xuan Loc in the face of an attack by 40,000 NVA. In the epic battle, the single most costly battle of the war, the ARVN defenders held off the attackers for an entire week. Such grim

The fall of South Vietnam, 1974–75

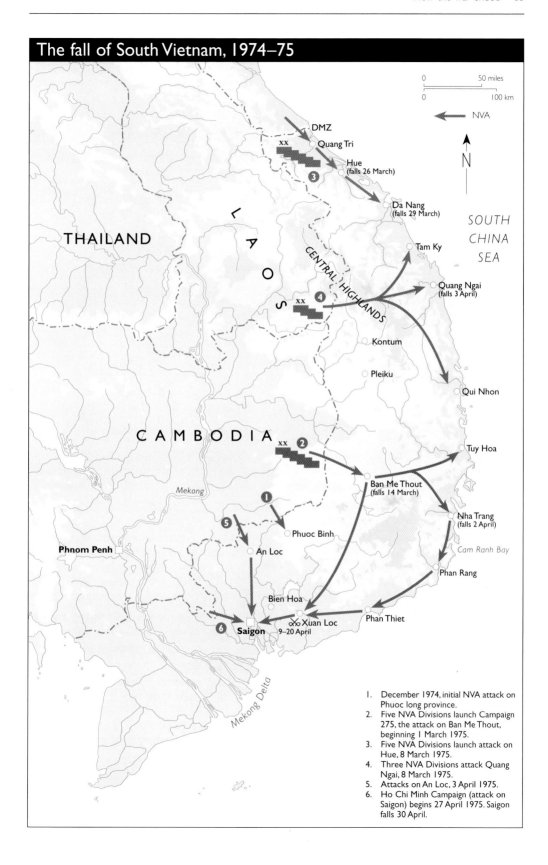

1. December 1974, initial NVA attack on Phuoc long province.
2. Five NVA Divisions launch Campaign 275, the attack on Ban Me Thout, beginning 1 March 1975.
3. Five NVA Divisions launch attack on Hue, 8 March 1975.
4. Three NVA Divisions attack Quang Ngai, 8 March 1975.
5. Attacks on An Loc, 3 April 1975.
6. Ho Chi Minh Campaign (attack on Saigon) begins 27 April 1975. Saigon falls 30 April.

Refugees helped aboard boats as South Vietnamese control over the Central Highlands of Vietnam quickly crumbles. (TRH Pictures)

tenacity in battle for a hopeless cause as the war drew to an end indicated the great potential of the ARVN, if only the political and economic ills of South Vietnam had been rectified in time. However, it was too late. Xuan Loc fell on 21 April, leaving the route to Saigon open. Realizing that the war was over President Thieu resigned, blaming the coming defeat on the abandonment of his nation by the United States, and fled the country a very wealthy man.

Amid ARVN defections and flight, on 25 April the NVA launched their attack on Saigon proper. At the same time US forces began a belated effort to evacuate those South Vietnamese who had been integral to the war effort. The experience of Hue in 1968 suggested that these tens of thousands of South Vietnamese nationals could expect little mercy from their conquerors. The evacuation, dubbed Operation Frequent Wind, rescued thousands by ships and aircraft – but as the NVA noose tightened around the stricken city US forces had to rely upon helicopter evacuations from atop buildings in the area even as rocket strikes shook the streets. Though many were saved thousands more were left behind brandishing papers allowing them to leave, only to face "reeducation" at the hands of the North Vietnamese.

Across Saigon resistance to the NVA advance quickly crumbled, leaving the communists to advance almost unopposed. At noon on 30 April a group of tanks crashed through the gates of the Presidential Palace, the symbol of South Vietnamese authority. Inside, the last President of South Vietnam, General Minh, waited to surrender to the victors. The ranking NVA officer on the scene was Colonel Bui Tin – a reporter for the NVA newspaper. Surprised to find himself taking part in such momentous events Tin strode into the palace to accept the final surrender of the government of South Vietnam. When Tin entered the room Minh said, "I have been waiting since early this morning to transfer power to you." Tin answered by saying, "There is no question of your transferring power. Your power has crumbled. You cannot give up what you do not have."

Legacies of victory and defeat

In many ways the Vietnam War was the most important event in the history of the late twentieth century. Years of combat against the Japanese, the French, the Americans and between themselves ravaged the nations of Southeast Asia leaving the area poverty stricken and in the throes of continued revolution and warfare. More importantly for world affairs, though, the consequences of the Vietnam War wrought great changes in America, the world's leading superpower. America had entered Vietnam as a powerful, united nation, certain of its cause and of victory. The defeat in Vietnam forced Americans to reassess their beliefs and values, and left the country battered and unsure as it sought to face the challenges of the final acts of the Cold War.

In its most simple and brutal form the legacy of the Vietnam War can be seen through the use of numbers. Those casualty figures are often inexact, they carry great relevance. During their war in Vietnam the French lost some 76,000 dead and 65,000 wounded – while their allies lost 19,000 dead and 13,000 wounded. Viet Minh forces lost an estimated 250,000 dead and 180,000 wounded, while civilian deaths from the fighting are estimated at 250,000. American forces lost some 58,000 dead and over 300,000 wounded during their involvement in Vietnam – 74,000 of the wounded either quadriplegics or multiple amputees. The latter number reflects the effectiveness of US medical efforts in Vietnam, for many soldiers survived who would have died in previous conflicts. South Vietnamese forces lost some 130,000 dead and 500,000 wounded. Allied forces also suffered losses with Korea losing 4,500 dead, Australia losing over 500 dead and 2,400 wounded, Thailand losing 350 dead and New Zealand losing 83 dead. The forces of North Vietnam

and the Viet Cong suffered the worst losing 1.1 million dead and 600,000 wounded during the fighting. In addition 330,000 communist fighters remain missing in action. Civilian deaths during American involvement in the Vietnam War are difficult to assess but run in excess of one million. In addition concurrent fighting and revolutionary atrocities in Laos and Cambodia led to the deaths of a further two million people. Thus during the conflicts in and around Vietnam that ended in 1975 nearly 5,000,000 people perished. That number, though, does not adequately express the cost of the war – for each fatality represents the agonizing grief of countless loved ones and friends.

The cost of victory

The victorious Vietnamese communists inherited a country that had been ravaged by 30 years of constant warfare. The infrastructure of the nation lay in ruins and millions of refugees wandered the battered countryside. More numbers put a human face on Vietnam's suffering. In 1975 Vietnam contained 200,000 prostitutes, 879,000 orphans, 200,000 disabled people and one million war widows. Amid the chaos the communist leadership went about enacting their long awaited revolution. Unexpectedly the purge of South Vietnamese society only resulted in the execution of some 60,000 "undesirables," while the majority of South Vietnamese supporters were sent to "reeducation" camps. Some underwent brutal torture at the hands of their captors, while most were only subject to indoctrination of a more subtle type. After a few years most prisoners began to emerge from the camps, but some remained imprisoned until the mid-1990s.

US forces attempting to keep order during the chaotic evacuation of Saigon. That 1.5 million people chose to flee Vietnam under such conditions demonstrates the extent of the Vietnamese economic and societal collapse. (TRH Pictures/US NAVY)

Economically Vietnam suffered from a botched attempt at agricultural collectivization, continued war and isolation from the west. Inflation ran high and with little hope of a better future nearly 1.5 million Vietnamese fled Vietnam in the late 1970s, usually by boat, seeking sanctuary in the west. Desperate refugees crowded onto any vessel that could float, hoping to make their ways into international waters and to freedom. Many perished in the attempt, sometimes even being captured by pirates, and thousands more only made it as far as squalid refugee camps in Hong Kong. Nearly one million Vietnamese citizens eventually reached their goal and made a new life for themselves in France and the United States. Penniless and without language skills the new immigrants, dubbed the "boat people," faced further struggles. Many were scorned as uncomfortable reminders of a lost war. With dogged determination, though, the Vietnamese immigrants became valuable members of the population of their adoptive homelands.

In neighboring Cambodia the Khmer Rouge put their own version of Marxist revolution into action by emptying the cities and murdering "intellectuals." Nearly 30 percent of the population of the tiny nation died in the orgy of slaughter known simply as the "killing fields." The Khmer Rouge nursed a bitter hatred of the Vietnamese and fighting lingered on the border between the two countries long after the close of the Vietnam War. In December 1978 the tensions exploded into open warfare as Vietnam invaded Cambodia. By 7 January Phnom Penh had fallen to the Vietnamese and the Khmer Rouge once again melted into the countryside to prosecute an insurgent campaign against a newly installed puppet regime. To the north China viewed the invasion of its client state of Cambodia with alarm. In an effort to exact a measure of revenge in February 1979 Chinese forces invaded the northern provinces of Vietnam – only leaving after having taught the

A lone soldier reflects among a grim reminder of the Cambodian "Killing Fields." (Topham Picturepoint)

Vietnamese a sufficient "lesson." The Chinese invasion notwithstanding, Vietnamese forces remained in control of Cambodia and would remain there for 20 years. Their presence in Cambodia was, though, in many ways counterproductive. The Cambodian incursion ruined warming relations with the United States and made Vietnam an international pariah state, ineligible for most forms of foreign monetary aid.

As a result of continued war and poor foreign relations Vietnam remained one of the world's poorest nations. In the 1980s famine stalked the land and inflation rates reached a high of 600 percent. Agricultural production continued to fall even as Vietnam achieved a 3 percent birthrate, one of the highest in the world. Facing societal destruction the Vietnamese Communist Party Congress announced a new policy of *doi moi*, or renovation, which allowed for the introduction of some aspects of a market economy. In addition the Vietnamese began to make overtures to the United States concerning the thorny missing in action (MIA) issue. Since the close of the Vietnam War the Americans had demanded a full accounting of the fates of MIAs as a precursor to normalized relations. In addition in 1988 the Vietnamese withdrew their troops from Cambodia. At the same time Vietnam's only supporter, the Soviet Union, began suffering its own period of societal change, leading to a 1991 decision to cut all economic aid to Vietnam.

The liberalization of policies in Vietnam, combined with the end of the Cold War, led to a rapprochement with the United States. American MIA teams were allowed to enter the country and by 1994 relations between the two nations were normalized. Slowly Vietnam began the process of modernization, but remained hindered by communist policies and a tremendously inefficient government. Though foreign investment is on the rise and Vietnam longs to become the next Asian economic tiger great problems still exist. The population of 75 million remains very poor, with a per

capita income of only $250 per year. In the end, though, it seems that a free market system will take over Vietnam and the hub of the country will move to Ho Chi Minh City, which its residents still refer to as Saigon. In a last note of irony, then, it seems to be the south, led by Saigon and its western ways, which will become dominant in a very different Vietnam in the twenty-first century.

The price of defeat

The United States had not been defeated in the truest sense of the term in the Vietnam War. No foreign invader had sacked Washington and the country remained the world's strongest nation. Also, as many Americans were quick to point out, American soldiers had never even lost a major battle during the entire course of the war. Such thoughts did not comfort most Americans, and only served to make the loss of the Vietnam War harder to bear. If the military had not failed in Vietnam it meant that the loss of the war was due to a wider failure of political policies and national morale. America, it seemed, had blundered. Its foreign policy had been misguided, its government had been less than genuine and its moral fiber found lacking.

The controversial defeat in Vietnam caused a painful, national catharsis in American society, which represented a sea change in American cultural history. Before the Vietnam War American exceptionalism had been alive and well. The United States was a good nation led by well-meaning people. In times of trouble Americans came to the aid of faltering European powers to save democracy from the hands of tyrants. Vietnam was different. America had been defeated; its leaders had lied; its soldiers had committed atrocities; its society had nearly imploded. It seemed to many that America had chosen the wrong cause and was not a savior in Vietnam, but a meddlesome bully. At the close of the Vietnam War America languished in a period of self-doubt and societal questioning. Many reacted to the failures of the Vietnam War by trying to forget them, contributing to the onset of the "Me Decade." The Vietnam War had crushed American exceptionalism and as a result America came of age. No longer would the people trust their government as they had before. Americans now saw their nation as one fully capable of making mistakes in a very confusing world.

After 1973 the political leadership of the country and the effectiveness of the military both fell under question. The effects of this national mistrust became known as the "Vietnam Syndrome." The public and national leaders were wary of using American military power overseas lest the resulting conflict become "another Vietnam." In 1983 President Ronald Reagan launched an invasion of the tiny island of Grenada, in part so the nation and the military would feel good about themselves again. In a bumbling attempt to make good its rejection of Vietnam veterans, the nation and the military lavished praise on the soldiers returning from Grenada. During the "war" some 6,000 soldiers fought a tiny battle against Cuban advisors. As a result the government awarded 8,700 medals. Though his tactics were sometimes brash Reagan did much to restore America's national pride.

The real test of the Vietnam Syndrome, however, occurred during the 1991 Gulf War. President Bush feared that the US would not accept high casualties and would not support a protracted war like that in Vietnam. The leaders of the campaign, General Norman Schwarzkopf and General Colin Powell, were Vietnam veterans. They had learned from their prior experience to enter a war with overwhelming force, achieve obtainable goals and exit the conflict. The resulting Gulf War was quick and ruthless, but also very limited in its scope, very much due to the lurking specter of Vietnam. Elated with his victory President Bush proclaimed, "By God, we've kicked the Vietnam Syndrome once and for all!" More recent events, though, indicate otherwise. Many Americans stood against the deployment of US forces in Kosovo, fearing a protracted war. Even in the wake of the terrorist attacks on the World Trade Center on 11 September 2001 questions abound concerning the coming war on terror. Will it take the shape of a "new Vietnam," and if so will the United States find the will to prosecute the war to ultimate victory? Vietnam, then, still carries a very real meaning and weight in American thinking and policy.

On the home front most Americans struggled to forget the trauma of Vietnam and the turmoil of the 1960s in an effort to get on with their lives. The war and its attendant social upheavals were over, and best forgotten. An uneasy sense of normalcy settled upon America as most people simply ignored the war and its consequences. As a result Vietnam quickly became the "forgotten war." In the process of the formation of this national amnesia the veterans of the Vietnam War were shunted to the side as unwelcome reminders of defeat and a time best left forgotten.

Unlike veterans of most wars, Vietnam veterans returned to their nation quickly and without ceremony. Single replacements left Vietnam alone, sometimes back at their family dinner table only 40 hours after leaving combat. Though they had only served one year tours the almost one million Vietnam combat veterans saw more fighting during their tour than the Second World War veterans had seen in theirs. These warriors were ripped from their combat units and rushed back into society without time to decompress, often with disastrous results. In addition Vietnam veterans returned to a society that did not welcome them home. They had lost their war and were sometimes met with ridicule, but were most often met with ignorance and apathy. Thus many Vietnam veterans, who had done only what their country had asked under tragic circumstances, found themselves abandoned and alone in a country that had forgotten them and their sacrifice. One veteran recalls his homecoming: "On returning from Vietnam, minus my right arm, I was accosted twice … by individuals who inquired,

A Vietnamese woman stands atop her houseboat in the Mekong Delta. Though still poverty-stricken recent economic reforms cause hope that Vietnam might become the next Asian economic tiger. (Author's collection)

'Where did you lose your arm? Vietnam?' I replied, 'Yes.' The response was, 'Good. Serves you right.'"

Rejection was made harder to take for Vietnam veterans because they could remember the great national welcome home afforded to their fathers after the Second World War. Vietnam veterans were denied the national support group so critical to their well being. They were young men (the average age of a combat soldier in Vietnam was 19) who had faced death, seen their friends die and participated in slaughter. Combat is a life-changing experience, difficult to deal with at the best of times. Traumatized and confused these young men found their sacrifice held unworthy of national notice or pride. As a result many

veterans began to close off from the world and dealt with the trauma of war in a destructive manner. Haunted by nightmares and the pain of war these veterans suffered alone for years, usually too proud to admit that they had problems. In a very real sense these men never returned from Vietnam.

For years the government and the Veterans Administration refused to admit that Vietnam veterans suffered any postwar problems. The professional psychiatric community only began to recognize their suffering in an organized way in the mid-1980s, and most veterans did not receive any treatment for their continuing problems until some 20 years after the war had ended. In psychological terms these men suffer from Post-traumatic Stress Disorder, which affects some 850,000 Vietnam veterans. In laymen's terms these veterans, though aided by new psychological techniques and care, are doomed constantly to relive their wartime experiences. One veteran recalls,

Even today, I feel like so much of me died in Vietnam, that at times I wished all of me had died over there. For those who came back, the price of living is never easy or cheap. Laughter and happiness is rare. The nightmares, the flashbacks, the pains, waking up soaked in sweat are the norm. The sounds and smells of combat, the smell of sweat and dust, of the damp earth and vegetation, of the hot sun and exhaustion, of ambushes and firefights to full-blown battles, and of blood and death, enter my daily life. The moans of the wounded, some cursing, others calling for their mother, someone screaming for the corpsman or moans of 'Oh God, Oh God.' Like so many other Vietnam vets, I feel so much rage in me that it exhausts me and isolation is my only sanctuary.

Half a world away the post Vietnam War national catharsis was echoed in Australia. Having fought hard and well Australian veterans too returned to a nation divided

Veterans and families at the opening of the Vietnam Veterans War Memorial in Washington – trying to achieve closure for a lost war and for societal rejection. (TRH Pictures)

against itself and struggling to come to terms with its own unique experience of war. After years of protests and a governmental shift toward the Labor Party, many Australians were only too happy to be rid of the Vietnam War and its attendant social discord. Once again it was the veterans of war, many returning to bitterness and rejection, who paid the price.

Australia and its Vietnam veteran population began to come to terms with a Welcome Home March in 1987 adn the dedication of a Vietnam Veteran's National Memorial in 1992 in Canberra. Though Vietnam caused Australia considerable national pain, it was an important part of the nation's maturation as a regional and world power, helping Australia to take the first steps toward a global role less reliant on the United States.

Times in both the United States and Vietnam have changed. Slowly Americans have come to terms with their lost crusade and now seek to make sense of the conflict. Belatedly the veterans of the Vietnam War are receiving their due praise. In Vietnam itself perceptions of the "American War," are

The Vietnam War becomes history. Here American students from the University of Southern Mississippi, meet with US and Vietnamese veterans in front of the Citadel in Hue – site of vicious fighting in the Tet Offensive in 1968. (Author's collection)

changing. The government is releasing its iron grip over information concerning the war, but change is slow. Historians in Vietnam still unquestioningly accept the party line of a glorious revolution. The change in Vietnam is perhaps best illustrated by the case of Bao Ninh. In his work *The Sorrow of War*, Bao Ninh relates the story of a North Vietnamese soldier in gruesome detail. Though recognized as a world classic the book is outlawed in Vietnam and the movements of Bao Ninh are tightly controlled. Even so his book is available on nearly every street corner, hawked to foreigners by ubiquitous street merchants.

As rapprochement between the two nations continues the United States and Vietnam will come to a fuller understanding of their violent, shared history. American businesses are flocking to Vietnam, attracted by its natural wealth and cheap workforce and undaunted by the bewildering

communist bureaucracy. This process threatens finally to bring a reluctant Vietnam into the modern age, posing serious concerns for a government that is hopelessly out of date. Along with businessmen American veterans are returning to Vietnam in record numbers, seeking to come to terms with their past. Young people of both nations, too young to remember the conflict but anxious to understand the experiences of their parents' generation, flood into classrooms to study the Vietnam War and its attendant history. In both nations universities and centers of study dedicate themselves to understanding the culture and history of their ex enemy. Some programs, notably at the University of Southern Mississippi, even take students and veterans to Vietnam as a group to meet with Vietnamese students and veterans seeking a shared understanding of the most important events of their lives. The Vietnam War, a conflict that ravaged several nations, left the world in turmoil and discord. The scars of war were so bad that only now, some 27 years after the fall of Saigon, are the first steps being taken to alter the enduring legacy of America's lost war.

Further reading

Baker, M., *NAM: the Vietnam War in the Words of the Soldiers Who Fought There*, Berkley Books, New York, 1983.

Becker, E., *When the War Was Over*, Public Affairs, New York, 1986.

Brende J., and E. Parson, *Vietnam Veterans: The Road to Recovery*, Plenum Press, New York, 1985.

Berman, L., *Planning a Tragedy: The Americanization of the War in Vietnam*, Norton, New York, 1982.

Cable, L.E., *Conflict of Myths: the Development of American Counterinsurgency Doctrine and the Vietnam War*, New York University Press, New York, 1988.

Croizat, V., *The Brown Water Navy*, Blandford, Poole, 1984.

Cutler, T., *Brown Water Black Berets*, Naval Institute Press, Annapolis, 1988.

Fall, B., *Hell in a Very Small Place: The Siege of Dien Bien Phu*, De Capo, New York, 1966.

Giap, Vo Nguyen, *Dien Bien Phu*, The Goi. Hanoi, 2000.

Farber, D., *The Age of Great Dreams*, Hill and Wang, New York, 1994.

Fitzgerald, F., *Fire in the Lake*, Random House, New York, 1972.

Gardner, L., *Approaching Vietnam: From World War II through Dien Bien Phu*, Norton, New York, 1988.

Isserman, M., and M. Kazin, *America Divided: The Civil War of the 1960's*, Oxford University Press, New York, 2000.

Jensen, G., and A. Wiest, *War in the Age of Technology*, New York University Press, New York, 2001.

Karnow, S., *Vietnam*, Viking, New York, 1983.

Khoi, Hoang, *The Ho Chi Minh Trail*, The Goi, Hanoi, 2001.

Lomperis, T., *From People's War to People's Rule*, The University of North Carolina Press, Chapel Hill, North Carolina, 1996.

Mangold, G., and J. Penycate, *The Tunnels of Cu Chi*, Berkley Books, New York, 1986.

Marolda, E., *By Sea Air and Land: An Illustrated History of the US navy in the War in Southeast Asia*, Navy Historical Center, Washington, D.C., 1994.

McNab, C., and A. Wiest, *The Illustrated History of the Vietnam War*, Thunder Bay, San Diego, 2000.

McNamara, R., *Argument Without End*, Public Affairs, New York, 1999.

Moore, H., and J. Galloway, *We Were Soldiers Once … And Young*, Harper, New York, 1992.

Moss, G., *Vietnam: An American Ordeal*, Prentice Hall, Upper Saddle River, New Jersey, 2002.

Murphy, E., *Semper Fi Vietnam*, Presidio, Novato, Califorina, 2000.

Ninh, Bao, *The Sorrow of War*, Pantheon, New York, 1993.

Nolan, K., *Into Laos*, Presidio, Novato, California, 1986.

Oberdorfer, D., *Tet*, Doubleday, New York, 1971.

Olson J., and R. Roberts, *Where the Domino Fell*, Brandywine Press, St. James, New York, 1999.

Plaster, J., *SOG: The Secret War of America's Commandos in Vietnam*, Simon and Schuster, New York, 1997.

Ross, R. (ed.), *Cambodia: A Country Study*, US Government Printing Office, Washington, D.C., 1990.

Shay, J., *Achilles in Vietnam*, Touchstone, New York, 1994.

Spector, R., *After Tet*, The Free Press, New York, 1993.

Summers, H., *On Strategy: A Critical Analysis of the Vietnam War*, Dell, New York, 1982.

Tucker, S., *The Encyclopedia of the Vietnam War*, Oxford University Press, New York, 2000.

Index

Related titles from Osprey Publishing

ELITE (ELI)

**Uniforms, equipment, tactics and personalities
of troops and commanders**

MEN-AT-ARMS (MAA)

**Uniforms, equipment, history
and organisation of troops**

CAMPAIGN (CAM)

**Strategies, tactics and battle experiences
of opposing armies**

ESSENTIAL HISTORIES (ESS)

**Concise overviews of major wars
and theatres of war**

NEW VANGUARD (NVG)

**Design, development and operation
of the machinery of war**

WARRIOR (WAR)

**Motivation, training, combat experiences
and equipment of individual soldiers**

ORDER OF BATTLE (OOB)

**Unit-by-unit troop movements and
command strategies of major battles**
Contact us for more details – see below

AIRCRAFT OF THE ACES (ACES)

**Experiences and achievements
of 'ace' fighter pilots**

AVIATION ELITE (AEU)

Combat histories of fighter or bomber units
Contact us for more details – see below

COMBAT AIRCRAFT (COM)

**History, technology and crews
of military aircraft**
Contact us for more details – see below

To order any of these titles, or for more information on Osprey Publishing, contact:

Osprey Direct (UK)   Tel: +44 (0)1933 443863   Fax: +44 (0)1933 443849   E-mail: info@ospreydirect.co.uk

Osprey Direct (USA) c/o MBI Publishing   Toll-free: 1 800 826 6600   Phone: 1 715 294 3345

Fax: 1 715 294 4448   E-mail: info@ospreydirectusa.com

www.ospreypublishing.com

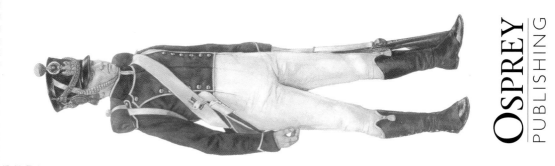

FIND OUT MORE ABOUT OSPREY

❏ Please send me a FREE trial issue of Osprey Military Journal

❏ Please send me the latest listing of Osprey's publications

❏ I would like to subscribe to Osprey's e-mail newsletter

Title/rank

Name

Address

Postcode/zip

State/country

E-mail

Which book did this card come from?

❏ I am interested in military history

My preferred period of military history is _____

❏ I am interested in military aviation

My preferred period of military aviation is _____

I am interested in (please tick all that apply)

❏ general history   ❏ militaria   ❏ model making

❏ wargaming   ❏ re-enactment

Please send to:

USA & Canada:
Osprey Direct USA, c/o MBI Publishing,
PO Box 1, 729 Prospect Ave, Osceola, WI 54020, USA

UK, Europe and rest of world:
Osprey Direct UK, PO Box 140, Wellingborough,
Northants, NN8 2FA, United Kingdom

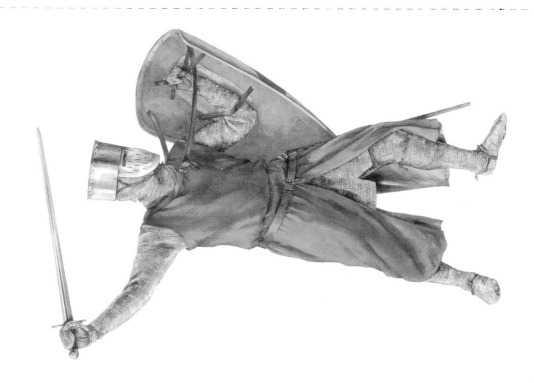

Young Guardsman
Figure taken from *Warrior 22: Imperial Guardsman 1799–1815*
Published by Osprey
Illustrated by Christa Hook

www.ospreypublishing.com

call our telephone hotline
for a free information pack

USA & Canada: 1-800-826-6600
UK, Europe and rest of world call:
+44 (0) 1933 443 863

959.7
WIE

Knight, c.1190
Figure taken from *Warrior 1: Norman Knight 950 – 1204AD*
Published by Osprey
Illustrated by Christa Hook

POSTCARD